S0-BKT-406

DARK AND
DASHING
HORSEMEN

DARK AND DASHING HORSEMEN

Stan Steiner

Harper & Row, Publishers, San Francisco
Cambridge, Hagerstown, New York, Philadelphia
London, Mexico City, São Paulo, Sydney

1817

Dark and Dashing Horsemen. Copyright © 1981 by Stan Steiner. All rights reserved. Printed in the United States of America. No part of this book may be used or reproduced in any manner whatsoever without written permission except in the case of brief quotations embodied in critical articles and reviews. For information address Harper & Row, Publishers, Inc., 10 East 53rd Street, New York, NY 10022. Published simultaneously in Canada by Fitzhenry & Whiteside, Limited, Toronto.

FIRST EDITION

Designer: Jim Mennick

Library of Congress Cataloging in Publication Data

Steiner, Stan.
  DARK AND DASHING HORSEMEN.

   1. Horses—History.   2. Horsemen—History.   I. Title.
SF283.S78   909   81–47420
ISBN 0–06–250850–4   AACR2

81 82 83 84 85 10 9 8 7 6 5 4 3 2 1

In gratitude to those who have by word or deed encouraged and aided me in the writing of this book:

Ray Allen Billington
Lazslo Borsanyi
Fray Angelico Chavez
Robert M. Denhardt
J. Frank Dobie
Seymour B. Leibman
Carlos Martinez Lopez
Nelson C. Nye
Arnold R. Rojas

Contents

Prologue: When God Created the Horse

When God created the horse He said to the magnificent creature:
I have made thee as no other. All the treasures of the earth shall
lie between thy eyes. Thou shalt cast mine enemies between thy
hooves, but thou shalt carry my friends upon thy back. Thy saddle
shalt be the seat of prayers to Me. And thou fly without any wings
and conquer without any sword. Oh, horse.

The Koran

Man was once a horse.

One of the most ancient stories of creation, that
of old Babylon, tells how the wise men thought
that the first man had become human. In the
beginning man was a wild horse, they said. He
lived in the forests with the beasts, as his father and
mother had done before him, for his parents were a
gazelle and a wild ass.

And then one day the horse-man of Babylon
met a beautiful and naked woman. She seduced him
and made love to him and he became human. Once
"the savage man" had learned to make love and

"lay on her murmuring the love she had taught him," her "woman's art of love" changed him forever. He was civilized.

Even so, he longed to return to the wilderness. He wanted to be a horse, not a man. He wanted to be as free as a wild horse.

"Now that you have become like a god," the woman chastised him with an admonition that sounds curiously modern, "why do you yearn to run wild again with the beasts in the hills?"

The man would not listen. He returned to the forests. But his old friends, the wild beasts, sniffed him and knew that he was human; and so "they fled from him." And the man, saddened by this, went back to the city where "he sat at the woman's feet."

The rites of passage to manhood and womanhood in ancient civilizations were often associated with the taming and breaking of wild horses, for when humans domesticated wild horses they seemed to domesticate themselves as well. The power and strength of the horse became human qualities to be sought and acquired. The esthetic appearance of the horse, its grace and beauty, was admired for the same reasons. In ancient literatures few animals are as lovingly described as the horse.

Strangely, the horse was seldom thought of as a deity by the ancients. It was seen as a servant of the gods, not as a god itself. The mares of Aphrodite and the stallions of Jehovah were depicted as heavenly steeds who served the gods and tested the humanity of humans; they had no divinity by themselves.

Many early cultures and religions believed that humans and horses were originally sisters and brothers. The Babylonians were not the only people who thought that the wild horse had been the original Adam. In the Hindu religion Lord Vishnu, too, declares that the first man appeared on earth riding a horse.

Still that thought was strange to me. I had forgotten the message of the Bible. In the Old and New Testaments it is written that the horse is the messenger of the Lord God. In Revelation does it not say that on the Day of Judgment the Almighty God would be seen riding across the heavens on a white horse? So it *is* written in Revelation, in the Bible: on the Day of Judgment, says Saint John, the Almighty God would appear upon His white horse and He would gather His armies of righteousness who "followed Him upon white horses" and so armed He would ride out "to smite the nations" and establish the reign of the Lord upon the earth once more.

God on a horse?

Yes. No human rode on a horse in the

beginning. The horse belonged to the gods; their power was awesome and frightening and few humans dared appear to assume it by imitating them. After all, one animal did not ride upon another animal, and weren't men and horses brothers?

In the mountains of Iran and on the hills of Galilee ten thousand years ago, when humans first captured and tamed wild horses, they changed the course of their own history. The feat was as momentous as the cultivation of corn or the discovery of love—it altered human existence.

For thousands of years horses were thought to pull the chariots of the sun and moon across the heavens. They were the celestial spaceships of ancient religions. They were the heralds of the gods. And, later, on earth they carried the armies of great empires upon their backs; they became the most advanced instrument of technology known to humans for many millennia, the machines of communication and transportation for most of the world's greatest civilizations.

Man-made machines such as airplanes and automobiles have existed for merely one hundred years. We have forgotten.

None of these things were in my mind when I began to write this book. And their realization

startled me as much as it may the reader who comes with me on my journey into the history of horses and horsemen and women, and the ways they have shaped human history; it is a strange journey and one that I did not plan to undertake.

My thought in the beginning was to write about John Wayne. The image of a man on a horse has loomed larger than life in our western history. I wished to search for the origin of the western horseman, western horse, western gear, western riding styles, western legends, western life. So often the heroes on horseback who have become a symbol of what is unique in the history of the American West seem to have appeared as upon a movie screen—suddenly and fully grown, as if they were born from their own ears; they seem to have no history and no immediate ancestors.

Nonsense. These horsemen and their horses have an ancestry that is as rich and complex as any history of the past. They have a heritage both as noble and as ignoble as any other lineage. But when I began the search for it I did not know where to look.

In my childhood the first horse I knew was a weary, sorrowful old swayback who pulled a neighborhood ice wagon we kids stole rides on. He was no messenger of the gods and no John Wayne ever rode on him!

And the farm horses I knew in the country were no more godlike. They worked hard, were sweaty, smelled of manure, and were covered with flies. No one rode on those old nags either. They didn't like to be sat on—by anyone.

When I was ten I saw a horse die pulling a farm wagon. I remember its carcass lying there in the road. The body of that dead horse was sent to a dog food company, not to heaven, and the farmer replaced his horse with a truck.

Sometimes I can see the same sad demise for the automobile that has befallen the horse. In the coming century as petroleum disappears from the earth so will the automobile as we know it, cherish it, and adore it.

The rituals of the automotive age may become mythological memories like those of the earlier era of horsemanship. No longer will our fondly remembered rites of passage to manhood or womanhood, from the ceremonies of initiation at puberty to the discovery of first love, be practiced in the sanctity of automobiles.

And yet, when that happens, may not the automobile become even more powerful in memory than it has been in reality—much as the image of the horse has become an enduring and romantic myth?

Of course, as a child I remember hearing of those romantic horses—the steeds of the Arabian

nights, the Asian horses of the Golden Horde, the
Berber stallions of the Jewish conquistadors, the
painted ponies of the Lakota warriors, the
mechanical horses of the urban cowboys of the
Hollywood movies. But these horses all existed in
my fantasies. They were not real. They had no
horseflesh, so to speak.

So in my search for the ancestral horsemen of
John Wayne I had to travel far back into history. It
was a journey that led me into the stables of
Solomon and on the caravans of Abraham; I rode
beside Darius, Emperor of Persia, and in the
mounted cavalry of Genghis Khan; I sat beside
Cortez on his white stallion and charged with Crazy
Horse at Little Big Horn.

There was no way that I could rediscover this
history of horsemanship without riding with the
equestrian legends—at least in my imagination. For
the truth is that these horsemen and their horses
have run away with my story. They have taken me,
almost unwillingly and certainly in wonder, through
a history I did not know existed, and they guided
me, not I them, in the telling of this story.

And so, in the end, I have simply tried to stay
on the historical horses, so to speak.

The old teller of horse tales J. Frank Dobie is
the spiritual father of this book. He knew and he
taught me, though we never met, that in telling the

story of horses you have to give them all of the free rein you can. If you don't they'll take it anyway. For history is as elusive as a wild horse, and a historian ought to try to stay in the saddle and ride it gently without attempting to break its spirit.

Dobie, in his history *The Mustangs,* begins by quoting Aristotle. The Greek philosopher said, "The artistic representation of history is a more serious pursuit than the exact writing of history, for the art of letters goes to the heart of things. . . ." And Dobie, having quoted the wise man, at once casts doubt upon his wisdom, as was his fashion. "Perhaps no writer could get to the heart of life by sticking to horses," Dobie says. "I don't know."

Now I don't know any more than Dobie did about "the heart of life," and I know considerably less than he did about horses, but I think he may have been both too modest and reverent at the same time.

As I see it, the history of horses, until this century, has been interlinked with the history of humans. They cannot be separated. This may be more true for men than women, but even that fact is interesting cause for comment.

So much of how men have seen themselves and thought of their manhood throughout history, the shapes it has taken and the meanings they have given it, has been expressed by the qualities of manhood they have given their horses and have taken from their horses. Even the idea of freedom, of manly freedom from society, has so often been tied to the imagery of the wild horse who forever roams free, untamed and unbroken by society.

And so, if the honor of a man exists "in a straw," as Shakespeare writes, why not write the history of man in the history of the horse?

1 The Old Testament Cowboys

On the Exodus from bondage in Egypt the Hebrews are usually imagined as fleeing across the desert on foot. They are depicted as a motley and ragged band—old men leaning on staffs, women cradling their infants in emaciated arms, children in rags. We see a long line of shabby and straggly refugees escaping with their lives and little else, carrying their meager belongings upon their backs like beasts of burden.

Were there no horses and horsemen among the Hebrews? None?

In the Old Testament it is written that during those years before the Exodus Joseph had been gathering vast herds of horses for the Hebrews. There was a famine and the Egyptians had suffered

severe losses among their livestock. Joseph, who
had gathered great stores of grain, offered to sell
them grain for their starving animals. When the
famine became more severe and they ran out of
money, he agreed to take their stock in return for
food for themselves. So "they brought their cattle
to Joseph, and Joseph gave them bread *in exchange
for horses,* and for the flocks, and for the cattle. . . ."

Moses, when he led the tribes of Israel out of
Egypt, may well have ridden on one of these
horses; perhaps other Israelite leaders did as well—
it does not say. The armies of the Pharaoh were
after all made up of "all the horsemen and chariots
of the Pharaoh and his horsemen"; it would not
have been easy to escape from so swift a mounted
army on foot.

To have fled on foot through the Red Sea and
the deserts of the Sinai may have made the
Hebrews' escape as foolish as it was miraculous.
They would not have gone very far by walking.
Nor does it seem sensible that tribal herdsmen and
shepherds would have gathered their flocks of
sheep and herds of cattle for the three- to
four-hundred-mile trek across the desert, but have
left their horses behind.

For centuries before the Exodus the men of
these tribes led caravans across the deserts from the
Euphrates to the Nile. They were renowned as

caravan masters as long ago as two millennia B.C.
Their beasts of burden, at that time, were often
half-wild asses and donkeys they not only had to
tame but train as well; so these Hebrews may have
been among the earliest bronco busters and
bareback riders.

These caravans of the desert, before the
domestication of camels about 1000 B.C., consisted
mostly of half-wild asses and donkeys, the famous
but infamous, petite but evil-tempered, scrawny but
strong "black donkeys" from Damascus. In the
Sinai and in Nubia there have been discoveries of
Egyptian documents from the nineteenth century
B.C. that tell of caravans of from three hundred to
one thousand donkeys. North, in Assyria, these
caravans were even larger, numbering as many as
several thousand donkeys in a single caravan.

The Old Testament scholar William Albright has
estimated that in biblical times "hundreds of
thousands of donkeys must have been required for
the innumerable caravans of the age." If that is so,
it could mean that there may have been thousands
of caravan masters and "cowboys" to herd the
animals among the Hebrews. Albright maintains
that the word for "Hebrew" comes from *apiru* or
abiru, which simply meant a "donkey caravaneer"
—a trail boss.

Asses and donkeys were not then thought of as

animals to be ridiculed as we might think of them today. They possessed the nobility that humans always attribute to creatures upon whom they depend for survival.

The importance of the donkey caravans in biblical history can be seen in the story of Abraham. In Genesis he travels on the donkey caravan routes and he lives in towns that were donkey caravan stations. He was described as a caravan master himself: Abraham, "the Hebrew."

Caravaning was a tough trade. The fierce donkeys, though small, were a sturdy breed that could carry 150 to 200 pounds each and go without water for two or three days. Even so, the slow and awkward caravans were repeatedly attacked by outlaws. "So the donkey drivers had to be fighting men as well," says Albright. In Genesis there is the description of the time when one of Abraham's caravans was attacked and he "armed his trained servants," all "three hundred and eight" of them, rode out in pursuit of the robbers, caught them, and his posse "brought back his goods."

Abraham was an expert horseman who would "saddle his ass" and ride into the desert, fearing no one but the Lord. He was what we might today call "a hard-riding man."

Not only were these Hebrews horsemen, but they were ranchers and stockmen as well. Abraham himself was a cattleman; he was "very rich in cattle," says Genesis. In seeking to enlarge his ranch he got into an early range war with Lot, a neighboring rancher. Grazing land was scarce in the deserts of Canaan—"the land was not able to bear them." So they and their ranch hands fought over "the plain of Jordan" that was "well watered everywhere" and there was "strife between the herdmen of Abraham and the herdmen of Lot."

In a lament as old as it is modern, Abraham said to Lot: "Let there be no strife between my herdmen and your herdmen; for we be brethren." But then as now, ranchers could be ornery and perhaps greedy when it came to grazing land.

So it was that Lot took his herds to the east and was separated from Abraham. The place that Lot decided to settle and where he set up his new ranching operation was a place named Sodom. At the time Lot knew nothing about the urban problems that would bring about its destruction; he merely wanted to graze his cattle.

On the cattle drives in search of new grazing land these biblical ranchers would bring along their entire tribes—not only all their people, but their own houses of worship as well. It was in this way that one group of nomadic shepherds and cattlemen created that remarkable mobile temple now known as the "Synagogue on Wheels," a temple carved from massive stones and set on a wagon with great wooden wheels resembling the covered wagon of the American pioneers. The "most ancient form of [Hebrew] temple," the scholar Ernest Munkacsi calls it in his *Ancient and Medieval Synagogues,* a "desert sanctuary." A stone carving of this nomadic temple can be seen on the crumbling walls of the Synagogue of Tell Hum near Galilee.

Many teams of oxen and horses must have been harnessed to pull the traveling temple through those desert sand dunes. The pillars and arches of the nomads' synagogue were carved out of solid rock; they most likely weighed several tons.

The "Synagogue on Wheels" was more than a testament to the faith of the Hebrew caravan drivers. It was a monument to their skill as wagon masters and stockmen.

Even when they settle in a farm or a village nothing is more important to a nomadic people than the care of their livestock. They live and die with their animals. And so when Jehovah commanded that the Sabbath be set aside as a day of rest He emphasized that He meant it not only for humans, but for their animals as well. Even "in ploughing time, and during harvest, ye shall rest," the Lord commanded the Israelites, "that thine ox and thine ass may rest" as well. The care of livestock was too crucial to life to be left entirely in the hands of the Hebrew ranchers—God included their care in a commandment to be followed as an act of faith in Him.

On the tablet of the commandments that Moses had been given on the mountain, the tenth commandment religiously declares the importance of a man's animals. No man may covet, it says, his "neighbor's house," or his "neighbor's wife," or his "neighbor's ox or ass." And similarly, when the Lord instructed the kings of Israel about their royal obligation He commanded that no king "multiply horses to himself" that belonged to another man, and that commandment came before the one that warned the king not to "multiply wives" of another man.

In the Old Testament the horse is often portrayed as a vehicle of the Lord. The horse appears in many guises—it is the bearer of His divine blessings and His moral laws, the messenger of His salvation, the sign of the triumph of righteousness, and the cruel instrument of Jehovah's wrath and heavenly vengeance.

Saul, the poor farmboy, was in the desert searching for his father's lost horses when the Lord told him of his destiny, that he was to be a King of Israel. . . .

And Ahab, when he had pleaded with Jehosaphat for aid in the battle against the Assyrians and Aramaeans, received the reply: "I am as thou art, my people as thy people, my horses as thy horses. . . ."

And Jezebel, the wife of Ahab, was punished for her blasphemy by being crushed to death beneath the chariot and horses of her own son's war general, and when the hooves of the horses had torn her body apart it was fed to the dogs to be eaten. . . .

And Jeremiah, when he intones the stern judgment of Jehovah on the hedonistic Israelites in 626 B.C., evokes the image of the Lord with the thunder of horses' hooves:

> Behold, like clouds He rises,
> His chariots are stormwinds,
> His horses swifter than vultures,
> Woe unto us. We are undone.
> O Jerusaleum, wash thyself of sin . . .

And when Amos cries out against the self-righteous hypocrisy of the temple priests of Bethel, he compares them to the false images of a horse:

> Do horses run upon craigs,
> Do you plough the sea with oxen,
> That you turn justice into poison
> And righteousness into wormwood. . . ?

And when Solomon decided to create "a settled place" for the nomadic Hebrews to dwell in, he ordered that "cities for his horsemen" and "cities for his chariots" be built. There he "gathered together [his] chariots and horsemen"; he "had one thousand and four hundred chariots and twelve thousand horsemen." And he had cities like these built not only in Lebanon and Jerusaleum, but "in all the land of his dominion."

For Solomon the "cities for his horsemen" were a symbol of his kingship, for a kingdom without horses was not a kingdom, and a king without horses was not a king. And so Solomon boasted that though he had three hundred concubines and seven hundred wives, could sing one thousand and five songs and he knew three thousand wise proverbs, he had twelve thousand horses. This number of horses conferred kingly status, wealth, and military power.

Solomon was nonetheless dissatisfied with his great herds of horses. Although he was a breeder of the finest horses, he was determined to further improve their blood line. So he had "horses brought out of Egypt" and he paid one hundred and fifty pieces of silver for each of these animals— evidently a high price, for the Old Testament records it with seeming disapproval.

And the horses of the King of Syria and the

King of the Hittites were brought to Solomon as well. In that time his stables inspired awe, for it was written that he had forty thousand stalls, one of the largest horse ranches in history.

The faith of the Hebrews in the moral and physical strength of their horses is perhaps best illustrated in the stories of Maccabeus. Here the horses are seen as heavenly animals, the right arm of Jehovah with which He protects His children, the Jews.

One day the soldiers of Timotheus rode forth on "horses out of Asia" to destroy Maccabeus and the Jews. But before the battle, as the sun was rising, Maccabeus prayed to the Lord for deliverance and in reply the Lord sent "from heaven five comely men upon horses" with bridles of gold to protect the Jews. And two of these were Jewish horsemen who "took Maccabeus betwixt them and covered him on every side" and they destroyed the "horses out of Asia." They killed six hundred enemy horsemen in all.

After the rout of Timotheus the king's cousin, Lysias, "gathered about fourscore thousand with all horsemen against the Jews." So armed he laid seige to Bethsura, a town near Jerusalem. Once again Maccabeus rallied his Jewish cavalry, and once again the Lord sent His horses of heaven to save the Jews.

"There appeared before them on horseback one in white clothing, shaking his armor," it is written. Inspired by this white knight of heaven the Jews "fell upon their enemies like lions" and slew eleven thousand soldiers and sixteen hundred horsemen and fourscore elephants.

For the horsemen of Israel to win a miraculous victory in battle it was not always necessary, though, for phantom riders on horseback to be sent from heaven by Jehovah. Sometimes the mere sound of the thundering hooves of the horses of the Lord was sufficient for them to defeat their enemies.

And so it was when the armies of the Syrians completely surrounded the Israelites. "The Lord had made the host of Syrians to hear a noise of chariots, and a noise of horses," frightening them so that they fled. For the Syrians "said one to another, Lo, the king of Israel hath hired against us the kings of the Hittites and the kings of the Egyptians, to come upon us. Wherefore they arose and fled into the twilight, and left their tents, and their horses, and their asses and fled for their life."

Quite understandably, the Israelites came to worship these heavenly horses of Jehovah. They repeatedly saw them in their visions of paradise, as did the prophet Elijah to whom they appeared as "horses of fire" pulling a "chariot of fire" that seemed nothing less than the "chariot of Israel." And Elijah, in a state of ecstasy because of his vision, rose in "a whirlwind to heaven" as his son Elisha, seeing the vision, cried: "My father, my father, the chariot of Israel and the horsemen thereof."

The prophet Zechariah, too, had seen the heavenly horses drawing not one but four war chariots across the skies. One chariot was drawn by white horses, one by red horses, one by black horses, and one by bay horses.

"O, Lord, what are these?" Zechariah asked.

"These are the four spirits of heaven," the angels said of these horses of the Lord.

For the horses of the Hebrews were not ordinary horses—they were the horses of the Lord Himself. And on earth their riders were religious visionaries who saw themselves as the horsemen of heaven on earth. The prophet Isaiah says: "Now the Egyptians are men, not gods, and their horses flesh, not spirits"; for it was the Hebrews alone who possessed the heavenly horses of Jehovah, the Lord of Israel.

No wonder that Mohammed, in the *Koran,* wrote that the Jews were people who appeared in "the likenesses of a horse, carrying books."

2 When Man Was a Horse

"Come to me, Gilgamesh, and be my bridegroom; grant me the seed of your body, let me be your bride and you shall be my husband." So the Goddess of Love of the Babylonians, the beautiful Ishtar, cajoled Gilgamesh, the king of the city of Uruk, as she attempted to seduce him. For to her his "body was perfect," his "manhood was radiant," and his "lust left not one virgin for her lover." And the Goddess of Love wished to have him, at once.

The manhood of Gilgamesh was so glorious she offered him the finest gifts she could think of, if only he would let her make love to him. She promised that all of his people would kiss his feet and all the rulers would bow before him and all of

his sheep would give birth to twins and his goats to
triplets and all of his pack-asses would run faster
than mules. Most of all, she promised him, if they
became lovers, his chariot horses would "become
famous in distant lands because of their swiftness"
—no one would have faster horses than his,
because her loving would make his horses ecstatic.

If Gilgamesh was at all tempted by these
promises of the Goddess of Love, he did not admit
it. He was scornful of her offers.

"And which of your lovers did you love
forever?" he asked coldly.

Many were her lovers and all of them had
suffered because of her. One man became blind and
another became lame; after she had made love to
them she rejected them and they were lonelier than
ever. He reminded her of what she had done to
the stallion she had seduced.

"After you loved the stallion who was
magnificent in battle, then you decreed whip and
spurs and thongs [reins] for him," Gilgamesh
recalled. "Then you forced him to run at full gallop
for seven leagues and muddied the water before he
could drink and his mother still weeps for him."
He would not be tamed and reined like that horse.

"If you and I were to become lovers, would I
not be treated in the same manner?" he asked her.
"You enslaved men with desires that were beyond

their reach," he said accusingly, and he turned his eyes away from her beauty.

The Goddess of Love was furious. In her rage she asked her father, Anu, the Father of the Gods, if he would lend her the Bull of Heaven so that she could with the vengeance of a woman scorned destroy King Gilgamesh as well as his Kingdom of Uruk. For Ishtar was not merely the Goddess of Love, she was the Goddess of War as well.

Her father, who talked like an old rancher, told her that if she did as she wished there would be a seven-year drought. And he was worried by what would happen to the people and their livestock.

"Do you have enough grain for the people and enough grass for the cattle?" he asked her.

"I have grain stored for the people and grass for the cattle," she assured him.

So her father lent her the mad Bull of Heaven who descended on Uruk like an earthquake. He created havoc. Gilgamesh seized the mad bull by the tail and thrust his sword between the bull's nape and horns like a matador and slew him; then he cut off the horns of the bull and hung them on the wall of his palace and had a feast in celebration of his triumph over the temptations of Ishtar. No longer did he have to fear the alluring and the threatening passion of the goddess who emasculated men.

"Now we can rest the night," the men of Gilgamesh said.

In her mourning, the Goddess of Love summoned all of "her people, the dancing girls and prostitutes of the Temple of Love, and all the courtesans of the city." "She set up lamentations upon the thighs of the Bull of Heaven," and all of the women wept.

One priestly poet whose name is unknown, during the First Dynasty of Babylon (about 1600 B.C.) composed a "Hymn to Ishtar." The "most awesome of the goddesses," he calls her; she is "the greatest of all the gods":

> She is clothed with pleasure and love.
> She is clothed with life and voluptuousness.
> Life comes from her mouth and her lips are sweet.
> She is glorious. Her body is beautiful.
> Indeed, all men and women must worship her.

"Among all the gods" she was revered because she was "supreme of all the gods," he wrote. She alone had created "the dwelling of joy" for man. Seen in that light the resistance of Ishtar's love by Gilgamesh would be all the more remarkable, for he had done what the gods could not do. He said no to the Goddess of Love and survived her wrath.

Gilgamesh, by his deed, became the first heroic man and the people hailed him—"A hero has appeared!" He was known as "Gilgamesh, the Godlike." The man who was human had defeated the woman who was a goddess. Now he would reign on the earth in her place as though he were a mortal god, the master of his fate, or so he thought.

And so Gilgamesh preserved his manhood by refusing to let Ishtar have a seed of his body. He had not been bridled and reined like the stallion she had seduced. He had not been tamed by love of this woman.

The "savage man," his friend Enkidu, was not as fortunate. His manhood was destroyed by a woman's love. In the forests Enkidu had been born of a mother who was a gazelle and a father who was a wild ass or horse. He lived with the beasts and chased "the wild ass of the hills." And to civilize him he was offered a girl, a harlot, who bared her breasts for him and laid aside her dress and he "possessed her ripeness." For seven nights and six days he made love to her. And when he returned to the forest "the gazelles ran off"; for he had become human, a tamed animal, and he had to go back to the city "to sit at the feet of the harlot."

So the "savage man" of nature became a civilized man who lived in cities. He was like a wild horse who was yoked to a chariot. The Babylonians believed that it was unnatural for a man of nature to live in a city; he had to deny his manhood to a woman, as Gilgamesh did, or lose his manhood to a woman, as Enkidu did.

The manhood so lost in the civilizing process could be regained only by the man becoming a warrior. He had to be the conqueror of nature, not live in love with her as Ishtar wished. He had to become a soldier on horseback, a warrior-hero.

On the barren deserts of Arabia and northern Africa horses were not native. They were brought into the valleys of the Nile and the Euphrates very early by invaders who had ridden in from the steppes of Central Asia, the savannahs of the southern Sahara, and the Indus River valley near the Sea of Persia. From the beginning, horses in these areas were synonymous with warriors and warfare, although the local peoples did not at first take up their use as cavalry mounts.

The domestication of horses by the Egyptians did not begin until the Eighteenth Dynasty of the New Kingdom (about 1650 B.C.) and even then they rarely rode their horses. Instead they used them to pull wagons and carry loads in desert caravans. There is little evidence in early Egyptian carvings and paintings of a pharaoh mounted on a horse—their fondness was for horses hitched to royal chariots.

The reluctance to actually ride on horses may account for the slow development of riding gear in the deserts. Even those who rode, expert horsemen like the Assyrians, rode without saddles and stirrups, although they had excellent bits and bridles and reins, equipment more necessary for guiding a horse harnessed to a chariot than for riding. Most of the horsemen of the desert tribes rode bareback or with the thinnest cloth beneath them. Their feet hung loosely without stirrups, although strangely, they sometimes wore spurs on their bare feet.

The early reluctance to ride may also have had something to do with the sacredness of horses, an idea that may have had its origins in their use as military weapons by the invaders. Men on horses were awesome war machines. A sword in the hands of a mounted horseman acquired a new and frightening power and lethality. It was not long after these war horses of Central Asia were ridden into the desert that they began to be worshipped as symbols of manhood, of kingship, and of the gods.

Sacrifice of a horse or ass was offered on only the most solemn and royal occasions—when a king had died, or a war had been lost, or a peace treaty had to be sanctified. Then and then alone might a horse be sacrificed.

On the tablets of Mara, found in the Palace of

King Zimri-Lim at Tell el-Harira, written in the old Babylonian of 1730 to 1700 B.C., an official wrote that he had "killed the ass [a horse]" to celebrate a treaty of peace between the people of Hanu and Idamares. In the diplomatic language of the time to "kill an ass [a horse]" meant to "make a treaty of peace," which was then solemnized by the sacrifice of a young foal to the gods of war and peace.

And as the horse was thought to be a sacred animal, the animal of the gods, the desert people may have been religiously hesitant to mount and ride them. Those who rode horses became men with the power of gods.

And yet like the Mesopotamians before them and the Assyrians after them, the Babylonians built their empire on the idea of man as a warrior. In the fertile valley of the Euphrates River there arose great city-states surrounded by mighty fortifications and guarded by vast armies of horsemen; for the civilizations built on the triumph of Gilgamesh were known for their legions of war chariots and war horses manned by armed warriors with which they conquered the pastoral villages and nomadic shepherd tribes of the deserts.

The cities that were early oases of urban life in the deserts were still separate and tribelike compared to modern ones. They were politically independent of one another and took on the particular characteristics of the tribal enclave. And so though these cities were urban in structure, the way of thinking of their inhabitants was still tribal in that every man in a city was expected to defend it; to be a soldier was one of the duties of citizenship. The French historian of ancient warfare Yvon Garlan, in *War in the Ancient World,* puts it succinctly: "A citizen [of a city] was by definition a soldier."

In the *Politics* the philosopher Aristotle writes that in the earliest republics of Greece citizenship was restricted exclusively to the horsemen in the cavalry. The honor of citizenship came to be judged not only by a soldier's heroism, but by his horsemanship. By the fifth century B.C. in Athens, citizens were divided into three censuses, or castes; only those belonging to the highest could serve in the cavalry, while those in the lowest had to be foot-soldiers. The use of horses by the soldiers of these city-states created a new kind of warrior society and warrior elite.

In the pastoral villages of farmers no warrior elite existed. On a farm the days were tuned to the rhythms of ploughing and sowing, growing and harvesting, and the seasons of the year. Survival meant living in harmony with nature.

So fields and farms that lay beyond the walls of the cities were rarely guarded or defended by their inhabitants, and the cavalry, considering them expendable, freely looted and burned the rural villages. They trampled crops and destroyed the harmony of rural life and the farmers of the villages hated them for it.

The soldier had a different view. His livelihood depended not on his being in harmony with nature, but in conquering it. He had to defeat the forces that stood in his way, natural or human, or they would kill him; they were his enemies.

Even the gods of the pastoral villages and the urban armies were in conflict. Of the earliest religious statues unearthed in the Stone Age farming communities of Jericho, Beidha, Ramas I, Tell Aswad, and Munhata, many are clay female figures that archaelogists now like to call earth goddesses. No less important and just as numerous are the clay figures of goats, boars, cattle, and horses that were most likely used in "magic rites to increase fertility of the herd or the hunted quarry," as James Mellaart writes in *The Neolithic of the Near East.* The pastoral and nomadic tribes of the desert worshipped the deities of fertility, of birth and rebirth, which seemed to them to be quite naturally represented by women and animals. Few clay figures of men were found, compared to the number of representations of women.

To the warrior societies of the cities the God of

War was most often a man. He rode across the sky in a war chariot drawn by heavenly horses. He was Gilgamesh, on horseback.

So, to the people of the rural villages and the warrior elites of the cities, horsemen were not the same men. Nor were horses the same animals. Men who once stood beside horses in harmony with nature mounted them and became conquering horsemen wielding the power of gods. Horses, once father and brothers of Enkidu, became servants of men.

The old Babylonian proverb sternly reminded horsemen: "After the horse had thrown off his rider, he said, 'If my burden is always to be this, I shall be weakened forever.' " So too in *The Book of Abiquar* in the fifth century B.C. it was written:

A man said to a wild ass one day, "Let me ride you and I will feed you."

The wild ass said to the man, "O, keep your fodder and may you never ride me!"

3 The Androgenous Horses

The Moon Goddess of the Oak Trees Cult was
Dia (Diana). Ixion, the son of Phlegyas, the King
of the Lapithes, had agreed to marry her, but he
was a vain and cowardly young man who became
frightened of his bride-to-be. As her husband, it
was said, his genitals would turn into mistletoe and
he would have to fertilize the earth with his sperm
and blood. So, understandably, he tried to back out
of the marriage.

And so the young man invited his future
father-in-law to dinner and killed him before they
were to eat, hoping this would cool the ardor of his
fiancée. It did.

Some said Zeus desired Dia for himself. He
disguised himself as a stallion and pranced about

her, flexing his enormous muscles until the Moon
Goddess could no longer resist his equestrian
erotics (horses were sacred to the moon); and so he
seduced her. They said that Zeus in his desire for
the goddess had played on the fears of Ixion and
had deliberately made a fool of him.

Be that as it may, Zeus was the Father of the
Gods and as such he was responsible for
rehabilitating the young murderer; so he invited
him to dinner. The boorish Ixion repaid Zeus for
his hospitality by attempting to seduce his wife,
Hera. She did not resist.

The old man, Zeus, read the intentions of the
young man, Ixion. And he created a cloud in the
form of his wife's body for the pleasure of his
dinner guest. In boyish enthusiasm, being too
drunk to notice the difference between a cloud and
a woman, the misguided Ixion fell with lust upon
the cloud (and most likely into it) and made love to
the imitation of Hera at the dinner table.

Even though making love to a cloud might seem
punishment enough, Zeus further punished Ixion
by having him tied to a burning wheel that was
doomed to roll through the heavens forever.

And then, perhaps to the surprise of everyone
concerned, the cloud became pregnant. The child
born of this ethereal mating was Centaurus, who,
when he became a man, mated with the mares of

Magnesia. Of those matings the mythic Centaurs, who were half man and half horse, were said to be born.

In the mountains of northern Greece there happened to be a real tribe whom the Greeks called barbarians, the Centauroi, the "People Who Speared Bulls" on horseback. They were feared horsemen whose riding skills both awed and disquieted the citizens of Athens. The Centauroi were considered uncivilized, the "ethnics," the Greek word for those who lived outside the walls of the cities. They were thought of as being no more human than their horses, as men who had "the lust of stallions."

No one knows if these tribal horsemen were the ancestors of the mythic Centaurs, or if they descended from the myth. In either case the Greeks portrayed the early Centaurs not as heroes but as bestial men, half-formed and ill-formed half-horses.

One depiction, seen on a Mycenaean gem found in the ruins of the Heraeum of Argos, shows two men facing one another, men who had grown rather crudely from the bodies of horses. Another representation on the walls of the Temple of Assos shows a man with the hindquarters of a horse.

In later centuries the Centaurs were depicted more gracefully, even handsomely. They were seen as horses with the full torsos of men, almost as if the men had emerged from the chest muscles of their horses.

Once the Centaurs had developed the bodies and souls of humans, they developed human passions but with superhuman strengths. And they became known as lovers. In their desire for human women, the Centaurs raided the wedding of the King of the Lapithes and attempted to steal the bride and bridesmaids. The battles that ensued became a favorite subject for painters in ancient Greece and in the Middle Ages who portrayed these Centaurs as heroic warriors.

So noble and handsome was one of these Centaurs by the name of Chiron, that he was described as a "Divine Beast." Heracles and Achilles had been his pupils; he taught Achilles to play the lyre. As well as a celebrated musician, he was a scholar of medicine, surgery, botany, astronomy, and hunting. When he died, the Roman god Jupiter placed him amid the stars where he reigns as Sagittarius, "the Archer," while in the constellations of the southern sky he is known simply as "the Centaur."

Centaurs were almost always depicted as men— all but once. In the volcanic ruins of Pompeii a bas relief was found in which a beautifully formed Centaur has the torso of a young woman. She is seen playing on a twin flute, enticing men to seduction, her horse's tail arched in anticipation, her hooves dancing to her own music.

In the end, as in the beginning, Centaurs came to be feared because of their licentiousness. By the time of the Roman poet Virgil, the once noble creatures were dispatched, in the *Aeneid,* to hell. There, according to Dante's *Inferno,* even Chiron, the "Divine Beast"—the "great Chiron whom Achilles had nursed"—was condemned to become the guardian of the "Lake of Boiling Blood" in the Seventh Circle of the Underworld. And Shakespeare later writes in disgust of the "stern and bloody" feasts of the Centaurs; he thought them "dreadful."

Like Pegasus, the Centaurs were doomed to fall from their godlike status. The Greeks had been ambivalent about them from the beginning, for a horse was an animal of the gods and an animal of the barbarians at the same time; it was to be revered and disdained, admired and ridiculed.

Musing upon the adoration of horsemen which seemed to fascinate and trouble the Grecian mind, the poet Sappho wrote wryly to her girl friend Anaktoria, who it is thought left her to marry a soldier:

Some say cavalry and others claim the infantry or a fleet of long oars is the supreme sight on this black earth.
I say it is the one you love.

And I for one would rather listen to your soft step
and see your radiant face than watch all the dazzling
chariots of the armed horsemen.

No one voiced the conflict between men on
horseback as the conquerers and builders of the city
states, and the horseless women whose love and
sustenance maintained human life in the city-states,
as simply and as succinctly as did the poet of the
golden-honeyed "joy of Aphrodite." She denied
none of the grandeur of the horsemen; she merely
bemoaned it.

Men, too, often felt both fear and awe for
horses and horsemen, as was sardonicly voiced by
Xenophon in his speech to his foot-soldiers. He
chided them for their fear of the cavalry:

If any of you is despondent because we are without
horsemen and the enemy has many, let him remember
that ten thousand horsemen are nothing but ten
thousand men. Nobody ever lost his life in battle from
the bite or kick of a horse. Besides, we are on far surer
footing than horsemen. They hang on their horses'
backs, afraid not only of us but of falling off. Horsemen
do have one advantage over us—retreat is safer for them
than it is for us, and faster.

On foot a man fought face to face, body to
body with his enemies. To be seated on a horse
was to hide from the heroism of battle. Not that
the Grecian armies did not make use of the cavalry

and war chariots. They are described in the *Iliad* of Homer where the wise old Nestor is said to have used them in a military maneuver similar to the one Jehovah employed in the battle of Maccabeus against Timotheus. And so did men learn warfare from their gods, as Homer writes:

First he arrayed the horsemen with their horses and chariots and behind them the infantry, many of them brave, to be the bulwark of the battle, but the cowards he drove into the center so that [they,] no matter how unwilling to fight, would of necessity have to fight. . . .

And yet in the *Iliad* the use of war chariots is belittled by Homer; he describes them as mere taxis. The warrior rode to the battlefield in his chariot, parked it, fought on foot, then returned to his chariot when the battle was over and he needed a ride home. One military historian thinks that Homer had only the "vaguest memory" of what a war chariot was for, but the poet might have been voicing the popular belief that a man in battle offered his body to the gods; he did not hide behind his horse.

The idolizing of horses may have seemed an uncivilized and backward passion to the men of Greece. It was an unwanted reminder of the tribal beliefs of their ancestors. Even worse, it was homage to the feminine deities of nature, for the adoration of horses had been integral to the

worship of the Moon Goddess and her celestial
court of heavenly horses who pulled her chariot
through the night skies. And it brought back
frightening memories of the days when Aphrodite
was protectress of the man-eating mares of
Diomedes, the King of Thrace, the mares Heracles
fought and the ones who devoured Glaucus.

People remembered these man-eating mares of
Aphrodite uneasily. In the story of Glaucus, the son
of Sisyphus, it is told how he had refused to let his
mares breed with stallions, "scorning the powers of
Aphrodite," and how by frustrating his mares'
desire for mates and love he hoped to make them
run faster in the chariot races. And to make his
mares as savage as stallions he fed them on human
flesh.

In anger Aphrodite complained to Zeus. She
wanted to punish Glaucus as Ishtar had punished
Gilgamesh in Babylon. Zeus agreed.

One night Aphrodite led these mares from the
stables of Glaucus to her sacred well. She grazed
them on the magical herb, hippomanes, growing on
the lip of the well. When the unwitting Glaucus
later yoked the mares to his chariot at the funeral
games for Pelias, the mares bolted, overthrew his
chariot, and dragged him, entangled in their reins,
across the entire length of the stadium. And then
the mares ate him up, flesh and bones.

It is said that to this day on the Isthmus of

Corinth the ghost of the devoured Glaucus roams the hills and haunts the horses. He is known as the "horse scarer."

The man-eating mares of Aphrodite became the symbol of an ancient conflict, not only between men and women, but the struggle for the reins of power, and succession to the throne. And they reappear in Grecian legends often to test the spiritual and moral strength, the manhood of men, as they did Heracles.

And yet, the Grecian mares, unlike the legendary stallions of older times, seemed to have been androgenous horses. They had both male and female qualities at the same time. They were mares, yet seem to possess life-taking qualities rather than life-giving ones.

Diomedes, the King of Thrace, had four of these man-eating mares in his stables. He kept them manacled with heavy iron chains and locked in stalls of solid bronze, for when they caught a man they would tear his flesh apart with their teeth and devour him in a sacrificial feast. The perplexed king in a futile attempt to quiet the hunger of his man-eating mares fed them on the flesh of unsuspecting guests he had invited to dinner.

And when Heracles, in his desire for immortality, offered to perform the heroic Twelve Labors of the Gods, he found the Eighth Labor was to steal the mares of Diomedes. He reined them and drove them to the sea. On the shore he fed Diomedes to his own mares and they ate him. Some said that he did this as a sacrificial offering to Aphrodite, who had risen from the sea. Some said by doing this Heracles was performing a new version of an old ritual, the sacrificial eating of the king, which in tribal times had been performed by women who wore the masks of horses and who "ate" the king at the end of his reign.

Once the mares had eaten the King of Thrace, it was said, they escaped from Heracles. They ran into the hills where they mated with wild stallions. But these mares who had lived on the flesh of men were no longer able to bear the flesh of horses, and after they were mounted by the stallions, they died.

Not so, says Diodoros Silculus, the historian. The mares survived and they lived for centuries on Mount Olympus, where they roamed as freely as later did the wild mustangs of the West.

4 The War God of One Thousand Horses

The God of War, Indra, is portrayed in the
Rig-Veda, the holy book of Vishnu, as "God of one
thousand testicles." The "male force," he is the
"fiery one"; he is "the strongest one who stays the
chariot wheels in battle, and he is the enemy of a
man who does not fight with all his might, and he
is a brother to a man who fights as a man." He is
Indra, the "terrible one," the "destroyer of all."
The phallic God of War, he is the "avenger."

Of all the gods of the Hindu religion he is the
most masculine. He is *eka,* the "one" who has the
"essential elements of manhood." And he is "alone
among men," he is "alone in the face of many," he
is "alone, by himself, without any help." In the
Rig-Veda Indra is identified in this way sixty-three
times.

No more ferocious and fierce military deity has existed in world religion. He is unforgiving, powerful, immoral, self-confident, and without remorse. "Strong by himself, a heroic one," he is "audacious in spirit, slaying men with a single stroke of the sword." The men on horseback who came from the Indus River valley and invaded the Fertile Crescent of the Middle East began their prayer to him before a battle: "O, Indra, the male force."

And no goddess could seduce Indra, as Ishtar had tried to charm the Babylonian hero, Gilgamesh, or as Aphrodite had done to so many gods. The manly God of War was beyond the reach of womanly love; he could not be tamed by a goddess or by a woman. He was inviolate.

In the second millennium B.C. when the horsemen of the tribes of the Indus River valley began to invade the plains of Mesopotamia and the plateaus of Persia they were protected by Indra. He rode with them, and he made them invincible, much as though he were an impenetrable armor they wore.

On the Persian plateaus he was given a new name. The magical Vereroragne of the Persians, the Acestian deity of triumph in battle, was merely another form of the mighty Indra. He was newly clothed in many guises that increased his potency tenfold, for he now had ten different bodies,

each of which was a form of the God of War. He
was:

> The wind, Vata . . .
> The ox who has "a force of aggression on his
> horns" . . .
> The lusting stallion . . .
> The camel in heat . . .
> The young man of fifteen . . .
> The wild boar . . .
> The wild ram . . .
> The wild he-goat . . .
> The swiftest bird of prey . . .
> The bird, Varanga . . .

And from the voracious example of these
creatures the Persian warriors learned how to fight.
Out of the combined strength and ruthlessness of
the many images of Indra they created a style of
horsemanship measuring up to the God of War
whose quintessence was his skill as a warrior and a
charioteer. It is written that Indra's war chariot was
"yoked to one thousand horses." The strength of
the warrior god of the Persians came, first of all,
from his horses.

The cavalrymen and archers of the armies of
Persia did not fight on the ground face to face, in
the manner of Homeric heroes. On the swift horses
of Asia, expertly ridden by the tribesmen of the

mountains, was developed a style of mobile warfare that Alexander later imitated. On the battlefield they pioneered the movement of vast armies with a maneuverability that the Huns and the Mongols were to learn from through the centuries, and adapt to their own styles of warfare.

Not merely did the Persians create a new style of horsemanship, they evolved the gear that was needed for its successful use in battle. Saddles that for centuries had consisted of simple, untied blankets tossed on horses' backs were replaced by saddles made of leather and wood, with high horns and backrests to hold the charging cavalrymen firmly in place. These saddles were tied with cinches around the horses' stomachs, a necessity if horsemen armored with shields and leather breastplates were to maintain their balance.

So saddled and armored, the horsemen could ride faster and be bolder. They rode higher in the saddle. They had more freedom with which to swing even larger swords. Equally important were the improvements they made in the bridles and reins that allowed greater control and maneuverability. The technological tools of horsemanship that the Persians developed were to forever change the relation of a rider to his mount.

Of all the innovations of the Persians, none had a more startling effect on horsemanship than did the lassos they perfected. Perhaps they learned the use of the thrown lasso from the herdsmen of their mountain tribes, for such lassos had been used by nomadic shepherds in many regions of the world long before the Persians developed them into weapons. And yet something as simple as a lasso made of a loosely held rope that was tossed freely had so great an advantage over the lasso made of a tightly knotted loop that was held like a snare; it revolutionized horsemanship by effectively extending the reach and grasping ability of the rider. In its time it was as remarkable an invention as the gas combustion engine or a missile to the moon is to us today.

All of the horse gear of the Persians developed from their idea that the horse was a servant of man and not of the gods. No longer were horses thought of as heavenly animals. If they were at all sacred, they were sacred to men and not to the deities. The domestication and use of the horse as a military weapon led to the secularization of the horse.

Man had become the master of the steeds of Jehovah; he possessed the power of the gods, as Indra did when he had yoked one thousand horses to his war chariot.

And so when one of the horses of the Emperor Cyrus was drowned in the Gyndes River, he ordered that the river "be punished." So, too, on crossing the Hellespont to do battle with the Grecian armies, the Emperor Xerxes ordered that his chariot be preceded by a chariot driven by ten white horses consecrated to the God of War; the purpose was not to calm the deity, but to assure a safe crossing for the Emperor. If the horses drowned Xerxes would be forewarned and having sacrificed his horses for his own well-being, he would take a different crossing.

To the Persians the horse and the horseman became closely identified. In mourning for a horseman killed in battle they cut off his horse's mane, as though it were the warrior's own hair, amid loud lamentations and funereal dirges. The Grecian historian Herodotus wrote in amazement of how they shaved not only themselves but their horses as well in their grief.

In the battle of Platera, after the Grecian armies had defeated the Persians in 479 B.C., Plutarch wrote that the Greeks judged the importance of their victory "not by the number of their enemies who lay dead on the battlefield, for they were few, but by the mourning of the barbarians who in their grief had shorn the manes of their horses and mules, as they had shorn their own hair."

And yet, the beliefs of men do not die as easily as men. The mythic power of horses as messengers of the gods continued to haunt the Persians long after they had mastered the horse for their own ends. They may have remembered, with some fear, the religious role of the horse in the legends of creation and death that the invaders from the Indus River valley had brought them millennia ago.

The nomadic invaders who had brought the use of horses as a weapon of war to Persia were the Aryans whom the indigenous pastoral people first called the "Daha" or "Dana," the "enemy," but who later came to be described as the people of "Eran," the area that is modern Iran. These Aryans settled and became the ancestors of the contemporary Iranians whose strong Moslem culture bears the mark of the harsh and warlike heritage on which it was founded.

But the Aryans did not dominate and populate the area by conquest alone. There was an affinity for the conquerors by the conquered that existed in the ways of living and of thinking of the original tribes of Persia, shaped as they were by life in that harsh mountain and desert area.

On the mountainous and stark steppes of the Middle East there had long been hunters of great skill. In the caves of Shanidar high in the Zagros Mountains of what is now northwest Iran and northeast Iraq there is evidence of human

habitation going back to 26,000 to 33,000 B.C.—
some say longer. The bedrock of one of these caves
reveals the telltale sign of possible human campfires
in the last glacial period, perhaps a hundred
thousand years ago. The Neanderthal families who
lived in these caves are believed to have hunted
wild animals such as the auroch, the ancestor of the
European buffalo, and the onager, a wild half-horse
and half-ass that originated in Central Asia and is
now known as the kiang horse.

The onagers were most likely hunted for food.
No evidence exists that these wild horses had been
tamed and ridden. Still, the appearance of these
horselike animals so early in the history of the
Persian highlands is testimony of the long
familiarity of humans and horses in the region.

Nowhere else in the Middle East have
archaeologists so far found evidence of Neanderthal
hunters that is as old as this, except in the caves of
the Levant in latter-day Palestine. But the hunters
there evidently did not hunt horses. So the
mountain tribes of Persia may have been among the
first to have become familiar with the wild horse of
Central Asia they called "the ass of the East," that
had come to their lands many thousands of years
before the Aryan invaders from the Indus River
valley brought its domesticated and trained
descendants as war mounts.

On the shores of Lake Tiberias, north of
Jericho, there is some evidence of wild horses at
about the time the desert tribes of Israel began to
herd gazelles at Ain Mallaha. That was about
10,000 B.C. And yet, it was not until four millennia
later, in 6,000 B.C., that the Natifian nomads of the
region began the harvesting of wild grasses to
obtain their grain as they herded wild animals.
Later still, in about 4,750 B.C., the cultivating of
wild grasses had begun in Kurdistan, near the
village of Jarma, in the highlands of Persia. The
domestication of animals, in both places, however,
is believed to have begun long before the
domestication of crops.

In the mountain villages of the Zagros range
near the old caves of Shanidar in the region that
now is the homeland of the Kurdish tribes, then,
some of the early human successes in harvesting
wild grasses and taming wild horses occurred. Some
historians believe the Kurds were relatively new to
the mountains and, being the descendants of the
Medes, a tribe of Aryan horsemen who had come
from the Indus River valley, knowledgeable about
taming horses. In the tablet chronicles of Akkad it
is written that the Guti, or Kurds, arrived in 2000
B.C. The Grecian general Xenophon (c. 430–355
B.C.) described his battles with them, as did
Artakhshir-i-Papakan, the founder of the Persian
dynasty of Sassanid, in A.D. 226. Neither defeated

them, and the Kurds remain largely independent to this day.

One thing alone is certain: when the Kurds settled in the mountains they mingled and married with the original inhabitants, descendants of the cave dwellers of Shanidar. And they were strengthened by the skills and knowledge of the people who had survived in these mountains from primeval times.

In the days when British rule dominated Iran, a political officer, E. B. Sloane, wrote of the Kurdish tribesmen as

"rapacious and furious fiends, fantastic figures of savagery, pouring out of the impregnable mountains and carrying desolation before them, slaying Christian and Musulman alike, resisting all efforts of the princes and powers to subdue them."

They were, Sloane lamented,

"shedders of blood, raisers of strife, seekers after turmoil and uproar, robbers and brigands; a people of depraved habits, ignorant of all mercy, devoid of all humanity, scorning the garment of wisdom; but a brave race and fearless."

That is, these mountain tribes seem to have eluded the inevitability of history—even the British Empire could not conquer and civilize them.

No horsemen seem to have as long a history of

mastery over horses as the men of the Kurdish tribes. The people of the region of the caves of Shanidar were not, however, as isolated and outside the mainstream of history as one might think in view of their apparent cultural integrity. In these mountains lay the Rowanduz River on whose banks ran the trade routes from Tabriz, Iran, to Bagdad, Iraq. And the nearby Zab River flowed past Shanidar to water the kingdoms of Mesopotamia and Babylon in the Euphrates valley, then as now.

The caravan routes across the Anatolian plateau of Asia Minor, by which the goods and ideas of Mesopotamia and Babylon once slowly made their way to early Greece, passed through these mountains as well. In those early centuries the caravans of merchants and missionaries came and went on camels and donkeys.

In later centuries, however, the Persians enlisted horsemen from the mountain tribes of the area in their phalanxes and armies of war chariots by the thousands to overpower the smaller legions of Grecian cavalry, at first sweeping almost all before them in their attempt to impose the culture of the Persian Empire on the Hellenic city-states.

On the "Royal Road," as it was known, the Persian horsemen of Darius and Xerxes traveled east. And, later, the horsemen of Alexander the

Great were to travel westward on the same route on their way into the Indus River valley. The civilizations of two continents were to clash here, and their battlecries to echo in these mountains.

5 The Wonderful Horsemen of Genghis Khan

On the undulating and unending sands of the Kara Kum desert to the south of the Aral Sea there lived a people named the Yueh-chih. They had been driven into the deserts by the Hsiung-nu, the Huns, who had defeated them, murdered their king, and turned his emptied skull into a drinking cup. Even then, in the second century B.C., the Huns were earning a reputation for dark humor.

The nomadic Huns were feared and fabled horsemen who had also invaded China and looted its cities. It was largely because of these barbarian horsemen that the Great Wall was built; the idea was that only a stone wall would stop a horse—but it did not.

Ever since the Chou horsemen had overrun the

Shang dynasty in the second millennium B.C., the Chinese emperors had been nervous about invasions of nomads from the east and north. The chariots of the emperors could "not withstand mounted archers nor ordinary towns the swift attack of nomad cavalry," wrote Oxford historian C. G. Simkin in *The Traditional Trade of Asia.* These nomadic attacks "forced the Chinese to become horsemen," but they still could not halt the ravaging of their cities.

And so the Emperor of China, Wu Ti, thought the Yueh-chih, who had suffered at the hands of these Huns, might join him in an alliance against them. He sent an envoy, Chang ch'ien, to persuade them, but the mission eventually failed.

Chang ch'ien's journey took twelve years. Like many a diplomat returning from a failed mission he told wonderful tales of his adventures to the Emperor to show him he had not come home empty-handed. Beyond the sands of the Kara Kum and the mountains of the Hindu Kush, in the lands of Darius, the Persian King, and Alexander the Great, there were great cities that possessed riches "splendid beyond description"; but most wonderful of all, he said, were the horses of these peoples, horses that "sweated blood."

"And I must tell your Majesty about the horses," Chang ch'ien said.

They are strange horses, unlike any you have even seen, for these horses sweat blood. And no other horses can compete with them; they are majestic in appearance and their hair is like silk and they are so clever they can understand what men are thinking and they are so strong they can gallop a thousand *li* in a day without any difficulty at all.

On hearing this the Emperor Wu Ti became quite excited. "The Son of Heaven loved horses," it was said of him. He not only loved them but he desperately needed them in great numbers for his army. In one of his campaigns against the Huns he used sixty thousand men and thirty thousand horses; so many were lost that after their victory his soldiers demanded the tribute of three thousand stallions from the Huns to replenish their own herds.

The Emperor sent Chang ch'ien back to the Yueh-chih to bring him those horses that "sweat blood." And so it was that the "Marco Polo of China" set forth to the West and "discovered the West"; he altered the course of history in search of a horse.

On the route that Chang ch'ien traveled to seek horses with which to fight the Huns the Hun horsemen were to travel, years later, on their invasion of Europe. And on that same route, on the same horses, the armies of Genghis Khan and Tamarlane were to ride forth in conquest.

For many centuries some of the most powerful and best trained horses in the world were bred on the deserts and steppes of Central Asia and the Near East. The endurance and tenacity of these horses was legendary, for some of them not only survived in a hostile environment, but seemingly survived the effects of history as well. It was in this desolate region that the Russian explorer Nicolai Przewalski in 1879 discovered the Siberian wild horses now named after him. A prehistoric animal scientists believed to be extinct, the *Equus przewalski* was a small horse with a large head and short legs that bore a remarkable resemblance to the horses of the Huns and Mongols.

Przewalski's wild horses were a testament to the remoteness of the region; their discovery was somewhat like finding a herd of extinct mammoths in the forests of Alaska. It was a testament to the perseverance and independence of these Asian horses as well as to the ecological balance they had achieved in so fragile and precarious a desert environment. Their survival was not entirely a miracle, however, for these horses had an affinity to the earth on which they lived. So did the men who rode them. Men and horses had a spiritual and physical sense of oneness that was almost familial, as though by living together for so many thousands of years they had acquired one another's traits and those of the earth that sustained them.

On the steppes of Central Asia that stretched from the Caspian Sea to the Altai Mountains there had once been neolithic hunters who had tamed wild horses as early as 4000 B.C. A vase from that time has been unearthed by Russian archaeologists; it is engraved with a procession of tamed animals, including two oxen, a boar, and one of Przewalski's horses of prehistory. There is evidence that these horses were not only tamed but were yoked to chariots and wheeled vehicles millennia before the people of Egypt, Mesopotamia, or China accomplished that monumental feat.

Some archaeologists believe that the armed chariot may have been developed by the horsemen of the steppes near Turan, in the third or second century B.C. The Chinese and Assyrians who used it early, and the Persians and Greeks who used it later, may have learned how from these horsemen of the Asian deserts and Iranian plateaus.

The nomadic horsemen who lived on the Asian steppes at the time of Genghis Khan's birth were not much more than ordinary herdsmen and pastoral tribesmen, who lived in separate small clans or bands. Each family group had its own khan, or headman. On those steppes and deserts, and in the

mountains surrounding them, there were hundreds
of these tribal bands of horsemen, perhaps
thousands.

One of the great and puzzling feats of Genghis
Khan was his achievement in forging an empire of
these tribes without creating a single nation as we
know it today. They were not all originally called
Mongols, that being merely the name of his own
tribe. There were also Merkits, Keraits, Naimans
and Tartars, and hundreds of other tribal groups,
united in an empire, but without a national identity,
a peculiar phenomenon of history.

Nor was the Golden Horde, as it is called,
really a horde. Its armies were not larger than fifty
to one hundred thousand men. They were almost
always outnumbered in battle, sometimes by as
much as five to one. Even the word "horde" is a
misnomer—it is derived from the Mongol word
ordu, which simply meant clan or camp, a tribal
gathering of an extended family.

And though they fought together for the Great
Khan, their loyalty was to their own clans and their
family khans. The fact that they often did not hold
on to the lands they had conquered, even after
their greatest victories, might be attributed to the
fact that they were tribal people whose loyalty was
first of all to their own lands—and horses.

The armies of the Mongols were armies of

individual horsemen. Almost every man rode; there were few foot-soldiers. To form a unified army of these headstrong and stubborn tribesmen on the battlefield was hardly an easy matter. And so the armies were meticulously trained in complicated maneuvers by holding war games called The Great Hunt that encouraged and utilized their individual skills as hunters, but taught them to hunt together by the thousands in formations that later became part of their disciplined and intricate cavalry attacks.

Because they could all ride and ride well, it was possible to execute complicated and effective battle strategies. They could strike swiftly and repeatedly, in sections or all together, and retreat just as quickly. More than anything else it was this mobility that made the armies of the Mongol khans seem invincible for so long. And their mobility was due to the horsemanship and horses of these tribesmen.

Each man, when he was ordered to serve, was expected to bring his "small herd" of horses. These horses belonged to him; he tended and fed them as he had done in his own *ordu*. And because each man had his "small herd," an army of fifty thousand men might have as many as a quarter of a million horses in its entourage—a spectacular sight.

If a soldier had only a few horses he might ride his mare; that way her foal and stallion would follow her. On the long marches his mare was essential to his survival in other ways; her milk and her blood would nourish him. But if a soldier had many horses he might ride his stallion knowing his entire herd would follow him "like dogs."

These horses were trained for warfare almost from birth. In the first years of their lives they were broken and ridden hard; but then they were put out to pasture for several years so that they could regain some of their independent spirit and strength before they were prepared for battle.

The Mongol horsemen tended their horses with great care. It was Genghis Khan himself who proclaimed the laws that governed the way his men treated their horses, including the decree that forbade the "leading of a horse with its bit in its mouth," and similarly callous acts of cruelty; his soldiers' horses were often treated more affectionately and humanely than were his soldiers.

And once a horse had ridden in battle it was a hero. It was treated like an old, honored veteran; when it became old or lame, it was retired to a grassy pasture until it died naturally. No one could kill a heroic horse even in human need, for example, for meat.

On the death of the horseman, and then only, was his horse ceremonially killed, to be buried beside its rider in a common grave. If the horseman was a nobleman, his stallion, a mare, and a foal were all buried with him, so that the horses might reproduce in death, and all of them—man and horses—would be forever fed on mare's milk.

At the funeral feast held in homage to the dead man and horse another horse was slaughtered upon the grave. The meat was roasted and eaten and the hide of that sacrificial horse was stuffed with straw and propped up on poles, as the Scythians had once done, so that it stood watch over the tomb, lifesize and lifelike.

All of these rites were practical and secular. The horseman and horse were not being prepared for a journey to heaven to be accepted by the gods. No divine spirit held the reins of the horseman of Genghis Khan. In the afterlife man and horse would simply live together forever as they had done on earth—solely dependent on one another for survival. That may have been why horses were buried fully saddled and bridled, ready to ride. Nothing could be left to the heavens and the horseman trusted no one—not even the gods—with his gear.

In life as in death, a horseman was responsible for seeing to it that his horse was well cared for; he had to carry his own food supply and equipment: a tool for repairing leather, a needle and rawhide thread, a fishing line, a cooking pot, a change of clothing, dried beef or jerky, and yogurt—all things familiar to an American cowboy except possibly the yogurt. But then the Mongol horseman *was* essentially a cowboy; he was one of the irreverent and down-to-earth horsemen.

On the horn of his saddle the cavalryman of the Khan had a lasso, a bit of military equipment borrowed from the Persians and still unknown in Europe. In battle he could use his rope with uncanny accuracy and lasso his enemy as though his enemy were a half-wild Asian cow. It was a fighting method that was to have a shocking effect upon the dignity of the knights of Europe.

It was not that these simple Mongol horsemen had better weapons or were better equipped than their European enemies. The technology of warfare was actually further advanced in Europe: men had gigantic cannons, heavier and more deadly weapons, armored horses that were like small tanks, and great fortresses and fortifications.

None of this technological weaponry was possessed by the horseman of the Khan. But his weapons were more effective because they were in harmony with his horse, not weighted upon him. His real weapon was the combination of horse and horseman, acting in unison.

Even the weaponry of the horsemen was fashioned to fit their horses. These cowboys had a small bow the size of a child's, but it was enormously strong; it had almost twice the force of an English longbow and could shoot an arrow for a fifth of a mile. By holding one end of the bow between his foot and his stirrup the Mongol cavalryman could shoot in any direction at full gallop, timing his arrows with swift and lethal accuracy in between the pounding hoofbeats of his horse.

The skills of the Mongol horsemen and the mobility of their armies were frightening and effective. In a short time they became not a few tribesmen raiding an enemy camp, but an army of a hundred thousand horsemen raiding the world.

These Asian cowboys on their agile but sturdy horses could easily ride circles around the medieval knights of Europe. Mounted on massive steeds that were bred to carry their heavy and awkward armor, these courtly knights were resplendent from head to foot in beautifully sculpted steel and gold. Unfortunately they were pathetic targets for the Mongol horsemen on their bold and quick little horses.

So the Knights of the Teutonic Order, the Knights of the Brotherhood of the Sword, and the Knights Templar all fell before these tribal horsemen like so many elephants. They were slaughtered during the Mongol invasion of Europe wherever they met in some of the greatest military disasters in the history of warfare.

No wonder the Europeans believed the Mongols were both less than human and superhuman. The Friar John of Plano Caprine, the Franciscan monk from Italy who was sent as an envoy of the papacy to the court of Ogedei Khan at Karakorum in 1246, solemnly reported that at the beginning of Mongol history "every woman had a human body and every man the body of a dog." Sons of dogs or not, these lowly men were so powerful, he said, that "It is their intention to overthrow all the world and reduce it to slavery."

In those lands they conquered the ruthlessness of the Mongol horsemen was terrifying; they burned entire cities, laid waste to entire nations, and annihilated entire peoples. They built nothing. They taught nothing. They squandered the treasures of civilizations. They destroyed almost everything they could not understand, though not in malice or for any religious or ideological reasons but as a matter of course—something that the Europeans could not understand either.

In fact, in their own homeland the Mongols encouraged and enjoyed a diversity of cultures and religions. The Friar William of Rubruck, a papal envoy to Karakorum in the thirteenth century, noted in amazement that a Christian church,

Moslem mosque, and Buddhist, Taoist, and Shamanist temples existed side by side, a sight that could be seen nowhere in Christendom or Islam at the time. But then was not Sorkaktani, the mother of Genghis Khan, a Christian, who to teach the meaning of tolerance to her son had endowed the Moslem University in the Holy City of Bukhara? Genghis Khan himself, it was said, favored the Christians, militarily if not theologically. His descendant, Kublai Khan, in fact sanctioned an alliance with the crusaders in the Holy Land to fight the Moslem Mamluks of Egypt and the Islamic Order of the Assassins. It is doubtful, though, whether either of these khans believed or disbelieved in any of these religions.

The defeat of the Mongol and Christian armies in 1260 at Ain Jalut, Goliath Springs, in the valley of the hills of Galilee where David had once slain Goliath, meant the end of the conquests of the Khan's horsemen. It meant the end as well of the dreams of the Holy Crusades. On their "blood-sweating" horses the Mongol horsemen retreated from Islam, as they had from Europe, back onto the steppes and deserts of Central Asia, no richer or wiser for all their conquests, pulling the shrouds of history over their memory.

Of the treasures of all the lands they conquered there seems to be only one thing they consistently preserved and cherished—the horses of their fallen enemies. The strongest and most beautiful of these they would capture and breed with their own beloved and indominable horses.

By this mixing the horses of the Mongols came to be a breed of breeds. There was the blood of Persian, Bedouin, Arabian, Chinese, Siberian, Hindu, Russian, Slavic, Magyar, and European horses in them. And then, in an unexpected cultural exchange these horses of mixed blood often found their way back to their countries of origin (or different ones) in succeeding campaigns of Mongol armies.

Unlike the other great military empires of the world, the "Mongols contributed little to the civilizations that came after them," writes the military historian James Chambers in *The Devil's Horsemen: The Mongol Invasion of Europe*. But he overlooks what might be the most enduring contribution of these Asian cowboys to the history not only of Europe, but America—their horses and horsemanship. For better or for worse, they introduced a style of mobile warfare, practiced on horses in their time, and on machinery in ours.

And so, during World War II it was not surprising that two of the greatest of tank commanders, General Rommel of Germany and General Patton, of the United States, both admired and studied the horsemen of Genghis Khan.

6 The Errant Knights

On a cool morning in April, 1214, Henry the Pious of Poland led a magnificent army of one hundred thousand men and thousands of majestically armored knights to a disasterous defeat by the Mongols. In that massive army were the finest knights of Silesia, Moravia, and Poland, and members of the Knights Templar of France and Teutonic Knights of Prussia—"the flower of northern European chivalry," one historian says.

On the plain near the city of Liegnitz the two armies clashed. The Mongol horsemen, battle-weary, dirty, and desolate, waited for the resplendent knights with their gold shields and silver swords, attacked them with their light cavalry in a shower of arrows, and then retreated. So small was the attack that Henry ordered the knights of the Duke of Oppeln and Teutonic Knights forward, where they fell into the trap set by the Mongols, who swiftly outflanked them with their light cavalry as their heavy cavalry thundered ahead, hidden by the smoke bombs they used to conceal the intricate maneuvers of their horsemen. The immobile knights were decimated.

It was a bloody massacre. The Prussian *Landmeister* of the Teutonic Knights escaped, but his knights were slaughtered. So were the Knights of the Templar Order, who died to a man. "The flower of northern European chivalry" was wiped out.

Escaping upon his horse, Henry the Pious tried to save himself. His horse, exhausted by the heavy weight of its own and its rider's armor, collapsed. And Henry, attempting to run in his suit of armor, was captured by the Mongols, who cut off his head and impaled it on a spear that they carried in triumph.

Amid the carnage on the battlefield, the Mongols cut an ear from each of the fallen soldiers and knights to count the dead. They gathered nine large sacks of ears in their body count.

After the defeat of the chivalrous knights, Friar Jordan of Giano wrote a precise account of the battle to the Bishop of Paris. He noted the mobility of the Mongol horsemen and highly praised the tactical maneuvers they used. But few in western Europe were interested in his objective military analysis. These Mongols were not considered human; were they not half-beasts and devils? Clearly there was nothing to be learned from them.

Solemnly, Ivo of Narbonne had written that their princes had "the heads of dogs" and their soldiers ate the bodies of the dead, tearing off the breasts of young girls, which were special delicacies to them. In Germany, the Mongols were said to be Jews, one of the Lost Tribes of Israel intent on destroying Christianity; in several cities Jewish merchants were hung in retaliation. And in France when Queen Blanche asked her son, Louis IX, what was going to happen, the king replied, "Either we shall send them back to hell, where they came from, or else they will send us to heaven."

More unnerving perhaps to the knights of the European orders with their codes of chivalry were reports that these Mongols had women soldiers who fought as fiercely as men. "She who fights the best is thought to be the most desirable," wrote Friar Jordan with the awe and unease of a celibate. These women, it was said, emasculated the men they conquered and ate their genitals. Even the Pope had cried out in alarm, "From the fury of the Tartars oh Lord deliver us!"

From throughout Europe there came calls for a New Crusade. But it was too late. The Mongols had all returned home to mourn the death of the Great Khan. With them went their style of skilled horsemanship and few influences remained to remind Europe of the Mongol invasions but the memories of the terrors they inflicted.

The medieval knights did not learn very much from the horsemen from Central Asia. Not that the cumbersome armor and lack of mobility did not make the knights envy and admire the agile horsemenship and mobility of these Mongols, but there were few ways they could adapt the skills of the tribal horsemen to their own manner of chivalrous warfare.

Nor was the gear of the Mongols of much use to the knights of Europe. They were not nomads. The short stirrups that enabled the Mongols to rise as swiftly as racing jockeys could not be used by the heavily armored knights who needed long stirrups to maintain their balance. The saddle horns that helped the Mongols ride side-saddle were equally useless. And the lasso that the Mongols tossed so effectly to dismount the knights was similiarly of no use—how could an armored knight throw a lasso?

Of least use of all was the Mongol's horse: that agile, tough, scruffy little beast. He was much too

small. The armored knight needed a large and tall
horse to carry his enormous weight. Large horses
were bred in Europe specifically to bear the burden
of a knight's armors and adornments. But the main
impediment to the adoption of any of the Mongols'
superior techniques of fighting on horseback was
not mechanical, but cultural.

Mongols were a dark-skinned, tribal and pagan
people; as such they were thought to be inferior to
the aristocratic knights of Europe. The lack of
chivalry of the Mongols was immoral and
unchristian and made them unworthy of imitation.
No lord of Christendom would easily admit to
learning anything from an infidel; that would have
been heresy, racial if not religious, for a civilized
man did not learn from an uncivilized one.

Actually, the gentlemanly knights need not have
thought it so incongruous, for their ancestors from
the Germanic tribes who ravaged Europe in the
fifth and sixth centuries were not unlike the
Mongols in the style of tribal horsemanship that
made it possible for them to overrun the Roman
Empire and Romanize their own tribal way of life.
The barbarians on horseback did not entirely
destroy the Roman tradition, but salvaged a new
way of life from its ruins, however. If the
Carolingian kings of the Dark Ages had not
accepted and utilized Christianity to build their

empire, would not the Franks have been remembered as barbarians?

Charlemagne the Bold, who has been called the "Father of Chivalry," was a son of these Germanic tribesmen. As a boy, it was said, he "gave himself eagerly to riding and hunting, arts which, as a Frank, he was born to." He sought to unify the warring tribes of horsemen into an army that was, in effect, little more than "a glorified raiding party."

In battle, the horsemen of Charlemagne fought much as the Mongols did. They took enemy prisoners as slaves or for ransom; when there was no ransom to be had they would slaughter everyone, as they exterminated the defeated Saxon army in 782, putting the entire army to death. Perhaps Charlemagne's ideas of chivalry, at best, have been somewhat exaggerated by those who came later.

Pope Urban, in calling for a Holy Crusade against the Saracens and the liberation of Jerusalem in 1095, invoked the name of Charlemagne as the symbol of Christian manhood. "Rise up and remember the manly deeds of your ancestors," intoned the Pope; remember "the prowess and greatness of Charlemagne." And so the crusaders set forth on their sacred pilgrimage for Christ in the name of a Frankish king.

Even so, the ideas of chivalry had their beginning in that dim time when Christianity became the religion of the semitribal horseman of prefeudal Europe. One of the early foundations of chivalry was laid when these tribesmen who in the 6th to 9th centuries vowed allegiance not merely to their clans and lands, but to Christ. Until the advent of feudalism, Europe was ruled by what the Germanic tribes called the *Faustrecht*—the law of the fist. The dictates of Christianity and the later codes of chivalry represented more than the establishment of brotherly orders of knights, for they imposed an organized system of sacrifice and absolution, of government and obedience on feudal Europe; in time they transformed the once tribal horsemen into knights.

The model for the knight was the Archangel Michael himself. His was "the first deed of knighthood and chivalrous prowess," said Jean Molinet. And from that heavenly beginning came the "terrestial knighthood" and "human chivalry." The orders of knights were no less religious than monastic or priestly orders. The Knights Templar considered themselves the Knights of the Temple of Jerusalem—the personal guardians of Christ.

And yet chivalry was a code for warriors, not saints. Though it is remembered romantically for its noble courtesies and acts of courtly love, it had its harsher aspects. In the twelfth century, the troubadour Bertrand de Born wrote of the proper manners for chivalrous knights on the battlefield as they fought for Christ:

And once entered in battle
let every man be proud of his birth,
think only of breaking arms and heads
for a man's worth more dead than beaten . . .

The code of chivalry served not only as a guide to the knights' etiquette of warfare—it justified and sanctified their "breaking of heads" by proclaiming that they did so in the name of Christ. So their brutalities in war were blessed by heavenly absolution.

Of equal importance to these knights, the code of chivalry protected them from each other. In face-to-face combat a single swing of a sword, mace, or lance could easily disembowel or decapitate a man. The knight who was thrown from his horse or whose horse died beneath him was pathetically imprisoned in his armor. By the chivalrous admonition declaring that if the knight took advantage of his fallen brother he disgraced himself before God both were saved.

In that sense, chivalry was less a moral code of Christian horsemanship than a code of self-preservation of the horsemen. The knight's life depended on his horsemanship; he was a nobleman, not a peasant, and the rites of horsemanship became the rites of chivalry, to both proclaim and protect his lofty status as the lord of his own fiefdom, his own nobility, his own soul. He offered to sacrifice himself to Christ, but he did everything to prevent that sacrifice from ever happening.

And the rites of war became the rites of love as well. Even as the knight knelt at the feet of his lord before going into battle, clasped his hands as in prayer, and swore an oath of fealty, so the lover knelt before his lady, clasped his hands as in prayer and swore an oath of fealty. The knights "equated courtliness and *manliness,*" as Meg Bogin writes in *The Women Troubadours,* for they put "war and woman-worship on an equal footing."

So the troubadour Peire Vidal sings of the affinity of war and love in knighthood:

> No matter what I do
> I look like a knight
> for I am a knight
> and in love I am master
> there never was a man
> so pleasing in bed
> or so savage in armor
> and so I am loved and dreaded . . .

The manhood of a knight was judged by his conquests. So too he judged himself. If his

---

conquests in battle were evidence of his manhood so too were his conquests in bed, for women too were to be conquered, whether by seduction or abduction. In his *Art of Love* the troubadour Guiart advises knights to take the women they love by force as proof of their love. "Manhood will honor you and God will delight," Guiart assures them.

Not that courtly lovers were not without the gentler graces, but a paradoxical part of courtly love was conquest by force. It was deemed a right of knighthood and women esteemed the men who forced themselves upon them as the thirteenth-century *Key to Love* explains:

So let her weep and whimper "rape"!
for she will not escape
even if she were able to.
No, no! She loves the derring-do;
Go to it. Love her on the spot . . .

Of all the places where the errant knights might find willing (or unwilling) ladies, none was more highly recommended than the fields for tournaments and jousting. The splendidly armored knights, festooned and adorned, risked their lives to exhibit their manhood and "chivalrous prowess" before the ladies of refinement who came to applaud not the spectacle so much as their display of manhood. And so, it was sung:

Where knights cross steel for king and court
showing their skill with manly pride
these tourneys, I repeat, provide
a fitting field for you who would
learn those delights of womanhood
for many a fancy wench abounds
round and about a tilting ground . . .

Love was a sacred act in the courtly tradition,
for all that. It was sanctified by God. Richard de
Fournival, in *Advise on Love,* declares: "I beseech
God in my favor that in days to come He may, in
His mercy, let me take pleasure in the delight of
love." And the troubadour Uc de Saint Circ
explicitly writes: "To be in love is to stretch toward
heaven through a woman."

And yet love itself was sacred, not the woman
loved. The courtly lover sang the praises of his
woman as he did his horse, but both were vehicles
he used in his quest of heaven and as evidence of
his manhood. Neither one did he consider sacred
in the way that ancient horsemen had done, in fear
and awe; a feudal knight looked upon his woman
and his horse as instruments of his conquests for his
own and God's greater glory.

The early feudal knights' ideas of courtly love
were as unsubtle and as brusque as their ideas of
manhood. But, unknown to the knights of Europe,

the refinement of some of their behavior and beliefs was influenced by an Arabian romanticism they despised.

In the early eleventh century a Spanish Islamic poet and scholar, Ali ibn-Hazm of Cordova, wrote the classic *The Dove's Neck Ring,* with its chapter on "The Submissiveness the Lover Owes His Lady." In it he exhalts women with a duality characteristic of Arabian love poetry that both idealizes and demeans them. His poetry was "at once more sensual and more spiritual than anything that could have come directly from indigenous Europe," says Meg Bogin in *The Women Troubadours,* and this "Arab influence was the single most important influence" on courtly love.

As the knights learned of Arabian horses during the Crusades, so they may have been influenced by Arabian romanticism. But they changed and adapted both of these to fit their feudal European mentality.

Guilhem de Poitou, the master of Provençal troubadours, had grown up "in the presence of hundreds of Moorish *joglares,* " the female troubadours of Spain. He began to write his songs after he returned from the Crusades, where he had been imprisoned for a year in the court of Tancrid. And so, too, the love poetry of Arabian and Andalusian horsemen of Spain may have influenced the thoughts of the troubadours and knights to the north.

One element of Arabian eroticism was curiously missing from feudal courtly love. The Arab poets often wrote in a female voice and many of their most sensuous poems were openly and passionately homosexual, an aspect of courtly love that was strangely unheard of in the known literature of "chivalrous prowess" of the wholly male orders of knights.

Chivalry was distinguished by its sacred vows of brotherhood. The codes of chivalry were after all for the benefit of men, not women, for nobles, not peasants. And the knights used their privileges as they wished in love or war.

The knightly orders could be brutal in enforcing these codes of chivalry. Peasants who dared to fight as heroically as knights were severely punished, for "the glory of death on the battlefield was reserved for armored men on horseback," says the military historian Alfred Vagts. In southern Germany when the peasants took up arms to defend King Henry IV in 1078, they were all castrated by the knights for "their presumption in bearing tools reserved for knighthood."

And a French chronicler of a battle in 1418 noted humorously that there was a nobleman who enlisted "a crowd of footmen, who all died" and there was "great laughter" for they were peasants, "all men of poor estate."

The knights' fear of the effectiveness of footmen was prophetic. The creation of new weapons carried by these footmen, the crossbow and the longbow, was to herald the death of chivalry, for they gave peasants an advantage over the knights in that it was no longer necessary to fight face to face. So great a threat to knighthood was posed by the crossbow that the Second Lateran Council in 1139 condemed it as "hateful to God and unfit for Christians"; it should be used only against infidels. By 1215 the crossbow had so decimated the orders of knights that nobles of England forced King John to include a provision in the Magna Charta banning foreign crossbow men from England's battlefields.

And if the crossbow threatened knighthood, the longbow doomed it. The longbow could be shot with such force and from so great a distance, that the foot-soldier could effectively shoot a heavily armored knight from his horse without becoming a victim of his deadly sword or lance. He was beyond the knight's reach and the knight was his easy target. Most vulnerable of all to the longbow was the knight's horse, the source of his strength.

Once a knight was unhorsed he was helpless, a pitiful figure stiff in armor, "a worm in a steel cocoon," they said, who was at the mercy of the lowly foot-soldiers. He could not get up. The foot-man had simply to raise the visor of the fallen knight and thrust his sword inside to impale the helpless knight within.

Knighthood was trapped in its own armor. Not merely more modern weaponry of manly warfare, but its own splendors and achievements doomed it; it collapsed under its own weight and became obsolete. No longer could these proud horsemen whose way of life depended upon their horsemanship even mount their own horses—they had to be lifted into the saddle by winches and hoists. The armor that was to protect them became the coffin in which knighthood was buried.

The death of knighthood in Europe was heralded in the disasterous battle of Crécy in 1346. In his invasion of France the English king, Edward III, brought a vast army of five thousand longbow men. On the battlefield they faced "the flower of France's knighthood." England's archers "let fly their arrows . . . so thick it seemed like snow," said the chronicler of the battle, John Froissart, and the knights of France fell like peasants.

Fifteen hundred knights were killed. They lay in heaps amid the carcasses of their horses—princes, counts, and dukes. Even the French king's horse was shot from beneath him. The English archer on foot had inflicted the worst defeat upon knighthood since the victory of the mounted archers of the Mongol army a century before; the English lost but two knights and forty foot-men in the battle.

Mourning the passing of the nobility of chivalry in battle, the medieval historian Max Jahns laments: "In olden times he who let his enemy have equal arms received great praise and honor," for the horsemen of old had been "good knightly people." Now the "good captain" was the man who defeated a "handicapped enemy"; the ideas of chivalry were dead.

As the years passed the orders of knights with their codes of chivalry, jousts, and tournaments, holy crusades and oaths of fealty, courtly love and noble death would fade into history. They would return as myths, and the knights like feudal cowboys would loom larger in memory than they had in life.

"Oh, ye knights of England! where is the custom and usage of noble chivalry that was used in the old days? What do you now but go to the baths and play at dice?" writes William Caxton in his eulogy *The Order of Chivalry* in 1484. "How many knights be there now in England that have the use and the exercise of a knight? That is, to wit, that he knows his horse and his horse him."

"There ye shall see manhood," Caxton says.

7 Romantic Horsemen of Spain

The romance of the medieval Spaniard began with his love of his own manhood; he was enthralled by the masculine imagery of his chivalry. In the same manner he idealized the feminine purity of the women he loved and demanded their virginity. After all, was not an early version of the paradoxical Don Juan legend written by Gabriel Téllez in Seville? He, too, sought the purity of love in a land where there was no purity.

Europe in the Dark Ages was largely isolated from the world; trade went on but there were few bold adventurers who went beyond the limits of its dark shores. The people turned inward and developed an almost provincial purity of beliefs and customs.

Not so Spain. There existed no feudal land with a greater mixture of cultures and peoples. The Islamic invasion that began in the seventh century and lasted for seven centuries opened the country to the migration of vast numbers of Moors, Arabs, Jews, Berbers, Egyptians, black Africans, Syrians, Yemenites, Byzantines, and Coptic Christians. These newcomers mingled with the older populations of Romans, Greeks, Phoenicians, Goths, Visigoths, Vandals, and the remnants of the Iberians.

And the invaders all came on their horses. They brought with them every style of horsemanship in the Mediterranean world and beyond, so that in horsemanship as in romance, there was no "purity" in Spain in all of its later history.

Still, the romantic ideal of purity played a part in the way in which the men of Spain explained their history. Even the Moslem conquest began, according to the legends, with an act of love that turned into an act of rape.

And so the tale is told:

Once there was a Byzantine prince named Julian who was the ruler of a Christian city near Tangiers in North Africa. He sent his beautiful daughter, Florinda, to Spain to be educated at Toledo. There, one day, as Florinda was bathing nude in the Tagus River, she was seen by Rodrigo, the King of the

Visigoths, who fell in love with her. And the king either seduced or raped the princess as she swam.

In a fatherly fury Julian, who some say was really the Berber chief Oulban, vowed to avenge his daughter's loss of virginity and in 709 he launched a boatload of horsemen to raid the coast of Spain and punish the king.

Rodrigo, it seems, was an unpopular ruler who had seized the throne over the protests of his nobles. The Spanish Jews also opposed him, for he denied them the right to practice their religion or livelihood and ordered them exiled. But the Jews refused to leave. They had come to Spain centuries before the Visigoths.

And so, a military alliance was formed between a Christian prince, who may have been a Berber, and the Spanish Jews, that eventually resulted in the Moslem invasion of Spain. The ships that carried the invading army were to be supplied by Julian and the invading army was supported and militarily aided by the Jews.

Of the twelve thousand men in the Moslem army that crossed the narrow Strait of Gibraltar from Africa, nearly all were Berbers. Few of them were Arabs. Some historians have estimated that there were no more than two hundred Arabs among them, and of the five thousand horsemen as few as twelve were Arabian. And the horses of "pure" Arabian blood were mostly Berber horses of motley desert breed descent.

So the Arab conquest of Spain was not very Arabian at all at the beginning. It was led by the Berber tribal chief Tariq ibn Zayid for whom Gibraltar, *Jabal Tariq,* was named; *Jabal Tariq* means the Mountain of Tariq. His Berber horsemen were the true conquerors of Spain in the year of Christ 711, and the year of Islam 89, who had the military aid of some Jews and Coptic Christians. The Arab armies did not land in Spain until later, after the Berbers secured the main foothold.

So decisively did the Berber horsemen defeat the army of the Visigoth King Rodrigo that after the battle of the Rio Barbate the king disappeared from history; he simply vanished. "Indeed, the Moslems found the king's white horse who was mired in the mud with its gilded saddle adorned with rubies and emeralds," wrote the Arab historian Ibn el-Athir, but all they could find of the king was "one of his half boots."

As the Berber tribesmen conquered city after city they did not have enough men to garrison the cities they had taken. The chief, Tariq ibn Zayid, requested that those Jews who volunteered to join the Moslem forces be armed, and it was the Jews who formed the garrisons of the conquered cities, fighting beside the armies of Islam.

In Cordova, Granada, Seville, and Toledo Jews were mobilized into the "Moslem militia." "That became the method of the conquerors," wrote Ibn Hayyan, whose words are believed copied in the *Akhbar madjmua* (one of Spain's most famous histories of the Moslem occupation): "In every city they took, the conquerors placed the Jews in the fortress to stand guard." And if the Germanic Christians rebelled, as they did in Seville and Cordova, it was the Jews who subdued them.

These Iberian Jews had lived in Spain since ancient times. In Andalusia were some of the oldest communities of Jews in Europe. A Spanish Grand Rabbi of the eleventh century traced their ancestry to the destruction of the Temple in Jerusalem, when the House of David came to Spain and settled in Seville. Among the exiles was not only the family of Ibn Da'ud (David) said the Rabbi, but that of Abrabanel as well (700 B.C.).

No matter what the exact historical time of their coming to Spain, the Jews were known to have lived in Andalusia for longer than the Greeks or the Romans. They were "Spanish" before "Spain" existed. And they thought of themselves as being more "Spanish" than the later "Spaniards."

Ever since the marauding Germanic tribes had

invaded the land in the fifth century, the Jews had armed themselves. For as Eliyahu Ashtor, professor of Arab Studies at the Hebrew University of Jerusalem writes in *The Jews of Moslem Spain,* the Iberian Jews were not like their brethren of the diaspora who took "no part in the wars of nations" where they lived. "The Jews of the Iberian penisula were proud and courageous, ready to draw the swords, and seize the spears," writes Ashtor; they had a "warlike trait." Nor was a military alliance between Jews and non-Jews unusual in Spain, he said. Even after the Arabs were in control of most of Spain "the Jews of Spain did not refrain from girding themselves with swords and going off to battle. They were accustomed to participating in war. . . ."

And so the swords of the Jews and the horsemen of the Berbers became the instruments of the Moslem conquest of Spain. The seven centuries of Islamic reign that followed were founded on their triumphs. So, too, were many of the traditions of gallant horsemanship and knight errantry that were to become part of the romances of Spain.

Of all the gifts the Berbers brought to Spain none was more important than their horsemanship. On the field of battle the small African horses of the Sahara ran circles around the heavily armored Visigoths on their huge European mounts. And on their high saddles and short stirrups the dark skinned tribesmen, whom the Spaniards called Moors, rode with a daring and swiftness that befuddled the would-be feudal knights.

The horses of the Berber nomads were not the magnificent Arabian horses of the legends, however. If there was anything noble about them, it was not they way they looked but the way they rode. A tough little breed of scrawny-legged, short-bodied animals with too-large heads, they appeared to be somewhat misshapen. But they ran with the agility of cheetahs, had the tenacity of mules, and they were as sure-footed as mountain goats—all skills they had learned in the sands of the Sahara where they had to have amazing endurance just to survive. In those shifting sands of the Sahara they learned as well to turn in mid-stride just to keep their balance, a trait their descendants, the *paso finos* of Puerto Rico and the quarter horses of the West, still possess.

Today these horses are known as Barbs, from the Barbary Coast of Africa (the shores of the *barbaros,* the barbarians, where they were originally thought to have come from). And yet little is really known of their historical origins, though it is assumed that they came from the biblical horses bred by Ishmael.

In the *Koran* it is written that the horses of the

Arabs are descended from the horses of Ishmael, the son of Abraham, who was as Mohammed said the spiritual father of the Arabs. Soon after Ishmael had been cast into the desert he came upon a wild mare, *Kuhaylan,* who was in foal. Excellent horseman that he was, Ishmael captured the mare and tamed her. He broke her, and when she had given birth to a colt he mated mother and son. From that coupling came the breed of horses of Islam known as Arabians. So the Arabs and their Arabian horses both owed their origins to Jewish horsemen—Abraham and Ishmael.

Not only their the horses but also their horsemanship may be something the Arabs got from the Jews. The Arabs were "the closest kin of Israel," writes Professor Goitein of the Hebrew University of Jerusalem, in *Jews and Arabs: Their Contact Through the Ages;* in ancient Hebrew the Arabs were often called *dodamin,* "cousins." "Islam is a recast of the Jewish religion on Arab soil," Goitein writes; so too the Arabian horse may have been bred from stock originally belonging to Hebrew horsemen.

Once, the Hebrews and the Arabs fought side by side, the Hebrews on horses and the Arabs on camels, for, in biblical times, the Arabs had few horses. They were still the People of the Camels and horses were not native to their desert or their way of life. It happened in the Battle of Karkar, on the plains of Syria, in 853 B.C. The mighty King Ahab of the Israelites gathered his army of two thousand horse-drawn chariots and ten thousand soldiers to halt the invasion of the Assyrians. And these Jewish warriors were joined in battle by Arab tribes led by the Sheikh Gindibu who fought beside the Jews with his army of one thousand camel drivers.

Even after Mohammed had built a stable full of horses, it says in the Koran that he did not entirely trust them. He decided to test their loyalty by depriving one hundred horses of any water for three days, and when they had been maddened with thirst he let the horses go to find water. As they stampeded he ordered that the horn of battle be blown. Most of the crazed horses ignored it; there were only five, all mares, who answered the Prophet's call and trotted obediently to his side. These five became the "Five Mares of the Prophet," his most loyal mounts, and their foals alone were honored by the name *asil,* Arabian horses of "pure blood."

At the oases of the deserts these horses of the Arabs were cared for by the women. In the Bedouin tribes women fed and groomed the horses, it was said, so that they became as obedient and loyal to a man as a woman should be. Like the

Babylonians and Greeks before them the Arabs seemed to recognize a similarity in the status of women and horses, for a horse was like a woman to the tribesmen of the deserts—it had to be a servant of its master.

The companionship of the Arabian horses and riders astounded the Europeans in Spain as they became more acquainted with them in the succeeding years of Moslem rule. In feudal Europe a horse was no longer thought of as a brother of its rider; man had been elevated to new heights by his chivalrous ideals and the horse, however noble, was still a beast. The familiarity of the desert tribesmen with their horses seemed pagan and primitive— almost indecent.

Even more astonishing was the style of riding that the desert horsemen brought to Europe. Knights rode *a la brida,* by the bridle, seated tall and rigid in the saddle, legs straight in long stirrups to support their heavy and awkward armor plates. And their horses, weighted and burdened, had been taught to charge straight ahead; they had no other choice.

One can imagine the bewilderment of the knights on seeing these other men charge past them like drunken circus acrobats. The Berbers and Arabs rode *a la jinete* or *a la gineta,* a style of riding that was halfway between a Lakota warrior and a horse racing jockey. In the manner of the *gineta* the saddle was set back with a high horn and backrest that held the rider firmly, so that if he leaned forward in his short, Mongol-like stirrups he looked as though he were kneeling in the saddle. And he held his horse in between his thighs so when he turned his body, his horse turned with him—he did not need a bridle. The *gineta* rider guided his horse with the touch of his hands, his knees and his thighs.

The name *gineta* for the riding style came from a Moorish tribe named the Zenetes who inhabited the desert mountains of the Sahara. It was an Arab version of a Berber word that was mispronounced by the Spanish, for it brought terror to the heart of a Spaniard. In the *Cronica de Alfonso el Sabio (The Chronicle of King Alfonso the Wise),* the armies of the Saracens were described as having five hundred thousand men, half of them from Andalusia and half of them Zenetes. And the *Historia de España* by Father Mariana describes how King John I of Castille died when his horse threw him because of the wild-riding Zeneta cavalry. And when King Alfonso III decided to defeat these horsemen he formed his own *Lanzas Zenetas,* the Zeneta Lancers.

Even Sancho Panza was honored for being *a la jinete* on a mule. The highest praise that one could give a Spanish horseman was to say he rode *muy jinete,* very *jinete.*

And so, much as the Spaniards despised and hated those they called the Moors, they emulated and admired them; and they imitated not only the horsemanship of their conquerors, but their way of life. "The climate of Andalusia softened the sons of these rude [Arab] horsemen," write Sir Charles Petrie and Louis Bertrand in *The History of Spain.* "It soon made them sensual and voluptuous, lovers of wine, singers and dancers, in short, [appreciators of] all the pleasures." And the Christians were "fascinated" by the Moslems, even if their church "severely condemned all carnal pleasures" and they had contempt for the Andalusian "paradise of houris and endless enjoyments."

So, El Cid cries out against the Moors: "I do not shut myself up with women, to drink and sing, as do your Lords!" He was, though he did not know it, the first Don Quixote of Spain, a man so utterly serious in his chivalrous and Christian pursuits he could not have known he would become a historic parody of himself.

And yet, seven hundred years of Moslem rule could not but change the Spaniards. That was especially so in Andalusia where most of the Berbers, Arabs and Jews settled and where most of the conquistadors who were to conquer the Americas came from. Waldo Frank in *Virgin Spain* writes with irony and affection of Andalusia: "There were Moslem lords whose ancestry counted

Visigoth and Jew; there were Christian bishops in whose veins flowed Yemen and Berber blood; there were Jewish poets whose mothers had been reared in a harem. . . ." And combinations of all of these were to become the "Spaniards" of later times.

In ancient times the tribes of Spain had been among the fiercest in Europe. "The Iberians were the most warlike of all barbarians," the Greek historian Thucydides wrote. But millennia of conquest by the Phoenician, Greek, Roman, and Germanic invaders had subdued and impoverished the original tribes of Iberia until the Jews and Moslems invigorated and revitalized their culture with a new spirit, and new challenges.

Moorish intellectualism and romance had a startling effect on the quiet, peasant society of Spain. The fierce sense of pride, the romantic machismo, the adoration of death, the foolish and courageous bravery, the celebration of sensuality and its religious denial, and the fanatical individualism—all of these were traits of the Berbers, Arabs, and Jews that developed from the characteristics once necessary for the survival of nomad tribes in the deserts—caused an upheaval in the cultural life of Visigoth Spain. And the Spaniards adopted these characteristics as their own, though in a feudal peasant society the heroic may have been ironic, the chivalrous may have been pedestrian, and El Cid may have become Don Quixote.

In the Cathedral of Seville, the Vatican of the Spanish empire, there are many multicultural symbols of that quixotic epoch preserved with the reverence of holy relics. Beside the bier where Columbus lies in a coffin carried as if in procession by four wooden courtiers, there is a sublime statue of a larger-than-life Christ of the Sorrows; he is nailed onto a wooden cross with a plaque over his head in which homage is paid to Him in Hebrew.

Not to be outdone, Ferdinand III, the "Holy Conqueror" of Seville who drove the Moors out of the city, has a plaque on his crypt in which his epitaph is proclaimed in Arabic, Hebrew, Latin, *and* Spanish.

The entire cathedral is a monument to the trinity of Moslem, Hebrew, and Christian Spain. Its exquisite tower, the lacelike Giralda, was begun by the Moslem ruler Abu Ya'qub Yusef in the year 1171, in memory of his victory over the Christians in the Battle of Alacos. But the Arabian historian Abdel Kslin says that the site of the Moslem minaret that is now the cathedral tower was originally built as a Jewish synagogue. It may be so, for the most holy Church of Santa Maria Blanca, the White Holy Mary, just behind the cathedral was a synagogue as well and the neighborhood that surrounds these churches was the old, feudal ghetto of Sevillian Jews.

On his conquest of Seville, King Ferdinand III ordered that the Moslem mosques and Hebrew synagogues be converted into Catholic churches. Inside the Giralda tower he had thirty-seven ramps built so that he could ride his horse to its pinnacle. And there, seated on horseback, two hundred and fifty feet up in the sky, he could look down on his kingdom below him.

In the massive and awesome interior of the cathedral the Spanish kings built perhaps the largest altarpiece in the world. The unbelievable altar was made of solid gold and was five or six stories high; it was composed of thirty-six lifesize tableaus of bibilical scenes of prophets and saints, all cast in gold that was originally taken from the temples of the Incas and Aztecs. So rich and ornate were the carvings and filigree work on the altar that it appeared to be dripping with gold.

At the foot of the gold altar there was a gold manger. Beside this knelt a gold-robed Mary and Joseph, while in the gold créche there lay a gold baby Jesus. Barely more than a few inches from the face of the Infant, as if blessing and protecting the Christ child, were the heads of two lowly farm animals. One was the long-horned Andalusian cow and the other was the head of a Moorish, or perhaps Jewish, horse.

The romance of the proud and "pure-blooded Spaniard," then, *limpia sangre*, was a magnificent and noble illusion from the beginning, but no less magnificent because it was human. For that hardly diminished the illusion. If anything the romantic dream was intensified in an attempt to make it a human reality.

8 The Jewish Conquistadors

On the eastern shore of Mexico where he
landed with his armored soldiers and horsemen,
Cortez unfurled the banners of the Spanish emperor
and implanted the Holy Cross of Christ on the
beach underneath the palm trees claiming all the
land in the name of Charles V, his Sacred Majesty,
the Potent Prince, the Most High and Excellent
Emperor of the Realm, and the King of Spain. By
his side stood his friend and fellow conquistador,
Hernando Alonso, a Jew.

Of those who came with Cortez there were six
known Jewish conquistadors. There were
undoubtedly many more, but these six were known
by name to the Holy Inquisition. Less than a
decade after they had charged across the land with

swords drawn and conquered Mexico in the name of Spain, two of these Jewish conquistadors had been burned at the stake, fallen heroes.

One of those who was burned alive was Hernando Alonso. He died on October 17, 1528. In spite of his fame and wealth no one could save him. His brother-in-law, Diego de Ordaz, was not only a fellow conquistador and a rancher second only to Cortez, but was the representative of Governor Velasquez of Cuba; he was therefore a man of great power at the court. In spite of his efforts on Alonso's behalf, a heroic Jew was nonetheless a Jew, and so he died.

The Jewish conquistador who marched beside Cortez was more than a conquistador. He was not just a conqueror, he was also a settler on the land— a horse rancher. And he was, perhaps, the first Jewish cowboy in America.

Eighty miles north of Mexico City, at the town of Actopan, Hernando Alonso established a cattle ranch, one of the first in Mexico, and there he raised cattle and supplied meats to the city. There, too, he bred what may have been the first foals born in the Americas. He was one of the earliest known ranchers in the New World, and his ranch grew large and prosperous.

Many of the first European ranchers, cattle growers, and horse breeders in Mexico were Jews.

The raising of livestock was not unfamiliar to the Spanish Jews, and since most of the conquistadors in the Cortez expedition were not interested in ranching—Cortez said disdainfully that he had not come to America "to work with his hands"—it fell to others to raise the livestock. And for the Jews who were in the land illegally—the Spanish laws prohibited any Jews traveling to the Americas—it may have seemed a safe and inconspicuous way of living. They came to hide from the laws. And once in America they disguised themselves as ranchers, something the Spaniards tolerated, at first, since they needed meat and grain as they themselves searched for treasure.

Even if the Jewish conquistadors had found gold, they could not have taken it out of the land. They could not return to Spain. And so ranching became a quiet refuge for these exiled Jews, who were the first cattlemen of Mexico and helped introduce cattle ranching into the American West.

They are the most forgotten and ignored of the dark and dashing horsemen, which is unfortunate, for their saga is one of the most exciting and significant in the history of horsemanship.

One of the largest of the cattle ranches in Mexico, Nuevo Leon, was established by Jewish conquistadors near Panuco on the Gulf coast in late 1579. In that forsaken region, two hundred miles from Mexico City, twice as far north as the Alonso ranch had been, more than one hundred Jewish families settled and founded a vast ranching operation.

Far from those intrigues and conflicts in Mexico City, these settlers probably thought they would be beyond the reach of the Holy Inquisition. That may have been one of the reasons Philip II of Spain granted them the land called Nuevo Leon—to isolate these Jewish exiles away from the Mexican capital.

Nuevo Leon was one of the largest royal land grants ever given by the king. It ran from the Panuco River northward across the Rio Grande, known then as the River of the Palms, onto the plains of west Texas, to the site of the present-day city of San Antonio—six hundred miles!

On May 31, 1579, the royal charter for Nuevo Leon was drawn up by Antonio Perez, the secretary to the king. Perez at that time served as the alter ego and, some said, the Machiavelli of courtly Philip, who signed it in the name of "God and me," as he liked to say.

The "empire within an empire" was given to the *hidalgo* don Luis de Carvajal y de la Cueva, who was to be its Governor General. He came from an old and distinguished family. One of his maternal uncles, Francisco Jorge de Andrada, had been a

Captain General in the court of the King of Portugal and one of his brothers was an influential monk in the Jesuit order. The Carvajals were a family of some prominence and stature in Spain as well. It was a Carvajal, Dr. Luis Galindez de Carvajal, a noted jurist, who was appointed Correo Mayor, or Postmaster General, of the Indies. And it was a Carvajal who was the director of the Casa de Contratacion, the omnipotent House of Trade in Seville that regulated all commerce to and from the Americas. These were gentlemen of comfort, and they lived an opulent and extravagant life.

In the Americas, the world of the Renaissance palaces and courtly trading houses seemed as distant as the stars. The lizards slid up and down the walls of their mud houses, and snakes lay coiled beneath their beds. And to a certain degree these wealthy Jews were going to have to live like Indians.

Panuco was no promised land. It too had its terrors. The forest beyond the beach was dark with real and imagined dangers. Not only were there the small, sleek cats, the ocelots and lynxs, but also the frightening jaguars and pumas.

In the dense growth of vines and ferns the darkness was almost impenetrable, even in broad day. And in that subterranean world there lurked poisonous snakes and vampire bats that awaited an unwary traveler. The forest was treacherous and deceptive; it enticed the romantic with a display of incredible beauty and then entrapped him like an animal. So, the land conquered its conquerors. Life was hard in paradise; it was "an uncomfortable and hot place," one settler wrote. And it was "full of mosquitos." The disillusioned Jews even had to walk "barefoot."

None of this was very new to don Carvajal, though; he came to the Indies in 1566 and gained some small reputation as a naval captain who had "fought against the Indians," though there is no record of his having done so. In any event, he had the proper credentials for a conquistador.

A man of dignity and courage, don Carvajal personally led the settlers to their royally promised land. He had, after all, financed the expedition largely by himself, as was the common practice of those given royal grants. The generous king gave them a beautiful piece of paper saying a part of the earth was theirs, but the rest was up to them.

The north country had been explored before by don Carvajal. He had lead several expeditions as far north as the Rio Grande in the 1570s. On these journeys, it was said, his soldiers had captured eight hundred to one thousand Indians, "for all the world as if he had gone hunting rabbits or deer," and had sold them in Mexico City as slaves, though Carvajal of course denied that he had engaged in the slave trade.

In any event, don Carvajal was as much an explorer as a conquistador. He may have been one of the first of the "Spaniards" to have crossed the Rio Grande and entered what is today the United States. If he did, he was surely the first Jew.

The strange and daring expedition of don Carvajal was unique in the conquests of the Americas. It resembled a quixotic "Ship of Fools." For among the conquistadors who sailed with him were such men as the son of the Viceroy of New Spain, don Diego Enriquez; Manuel de Morales, a Hebrew scholar whose father-in-law had been Grand Rabbi of Portugal before he was burned at the stake; Antonio Machado, whose house was used as a synagogue by the settlers and whom they called the *Gran Rabino;* Antonio de Morales, a Jewish doctor; and the families of Rodriguez, de Leon, Martinez, Hernandez, Marquez, Lopez, Espinosa, Nava and Juarez, all bearing Sephardic Jewish names; as well as almost the entire family of don Carvajal, who were later to be burned at the stake or banished as "secret" Jews.

By that time there had been a great number of "secret" Jewish emigrants to Mexico. There were *hebreo cristianos* (Hebrew Christians), *nuevo cristianos*

(New Christians), *conversos* (converted Jews) and those who were called the *marranos* (the swine). By 1545 one quarter of the Spaniards in Mexico City were Jewish. The royal census of that year counted a European population of 1,358, of whom, according to the survey made by the Marquis de Guadalcazar, 300 were openly admitted Jews. And that would not include the "secret" Jews. From these figures Francisco Fernandez de Castillo concludes, in *Libros y liberos del siglo XVI,* that in Mexico City "there were more Jews than Catholics."

In 1506 the Bishop of Puerto Rico complained that Portuguese boats arriving in the New World were bringing "mostly Hebrews." While in 1510 the Bishop of Cuba complained that every new boat from Spain "was full" of Jews, *conversos,* and "secret" heretics.

Even the father of the church and chronicler of the conquest Bernardino de Sahagun, a Franciscan monk, was born of Jewish parents according to Father Angel Maria Garibay, Canon of the Basilica of Guadalupe in Mexico City. And so too was Francisco de Vitoria, the Archbishop of Mexico, and the church historian, Father Diego de Duran, who was born the "natural son" of a *mestiza,* a half-Indian woman, and a Jewish conquistador.

So many Jews had come to Mexico that by the

1650s, one hundred and fifty years after the beginning of the Holy Inquisition, there were fifteen synagogues in Mexico City. And there were, as well, three synagogues in Puebla, two each in Veracruz and Guadalajara, and one each in Zacatecas, Campeche, Merida, and Monterrey.

And Jewish representation among the conquistadors in the colonies of South America was no less numerous. A sixteenth-century Peruvian writer, Pinto de Lima, estimated that seventy-five percent of the Spaniards in Peru were or had been Jews, while Laerte de Ferreira said that "Jewish blood" was common among all the conquistadors. In this vein the Spanish historian Salvador de Madariaga wrote that when the Inquisition exiled the Spanish Jews they "left behind a deeply judaized Spain and they went abroad no less hispanified."

Many, if not most, of the families of those conquistadors who came with don Carvajal were publicly and openly Jewish. They were "unrepentant" as the historian Leslie Bird Simpson writes, and the Holy Inquisition was to confirm this. For they were a people obstinate in their beliefs as well as in their pioneering spirits of survival.

Some of these reluctant Jewish conquistadors may have been swordsmen and horsemen in

Europe. In Mexico they all had to be—they had to
defend themselves against their fellow conquistadors
as well as the Indians.

Ever since the Spaniards had come to Panuco
they had fought one another for its possession. The
town was no more than a few mud huts, but its
harbor was one of the finest on the Gulf coast. The
remnants of the DeSoto expedition had sought
refuge there, as had the expedition of Grijalva in
1517, whose report of Indian gold inspired Cortez
to sail in search of treasure, a voyage that began
the conquest of Mexico. One of the first lands that
Cortez claimed as his own was Panuco.

Of all the slave estates that Cortez founded, few
produced greater revenue in gold and cloth than
Panuco. The tributes seized from the Indian tribes
of the area alone amounted to five thousand gold
pesos a year. These tribes also became the sources
of the slaves who were forced to work on Cortez's
estates.

No sooner had Cortez announced the creation
of his personal empire than he was challenged by
Governor Francisco de Garay of Jamaica, who
landed at Panuco with an army of more than six
hundred men and three hundred horses. They
surrendered almost at once in a battle unremarkable
except for one thing: in his chronicles of the battle
Peter Martyr, for the first time, mentioned the

great plains that ranged north from Panuco to
Texas.

And then there were the Indians . . .

When the Spanish came to Panuco they decided
to Christianize the native people. Somewhat
overenthusiastically Cortez named the settlement
Santiestivan, Saint Steven, and ordered the building
of churches. But the tribes did not look reverently
upon his endeavor. They burned the churches to
the ground.

In the royal charter given to don Carvajal the
resistance of these Indians was unhappily noted.
The new settlers were ordered by the king to pacify
these rebellious natives—or lose their charter:

". . . On the confines of Panuco territory . . . are
people [Indians] . . . formerly Christianized but for five
years they have been in rebellion, destroying churches
and doing other damage. The Viceroy has dispatched his
captains and soldiers to subdue them, but though they
have tried hard they have been unable to pacify
them. . . ."

The settlers were thus ordered to do what the
soldiers could not. "You are obligated to bring the
Indians to peace and Christianity," the royal charter
decreed. And this was to be done "within eight
years."

If the secretary to Philip II saw any humor in

ordering converted and crypto Jews to Christianize Indians the solemn wording of the royal charter offered no hint of it. Nor did the Holy Inquisition comment on the irony of this document.

Not many conversions of Indians to Christianity took place in Panuco, though don Carvajal did order the building of a church for them in Cueva. Whether any of these Indians were converted to Judaism was not recorded.

Some of the settlers were understandably dissatisfied with life at Panuco. The unrelenting heat and unending tropical rain of the river delta made them restless and disconsolate; they felt the atmosphere was oppressive.

And so the bolder of the Jews decided to abandon Panuco. They headed north into the mountains of Zacatecas and across the arid lands of Coahuila. In the Taramuhara Indian country they founded a ranching settlement of Monclova, south of the Rio Grande; it was the first ranch in the territory that was to become a breeding ground for the long-horned cattle and mustangs of northern Mexico and southwestern Texas.

Pioneers on the frontiers of Nuevo Leon in the 1590s, these ranchers who headed north then disappeared into history. Even their names are now forgotten. They left no memoirs. They kept few records.

Nothing is known of their explorations. If some may have reached the Rio Grande, as was likely, and crossed over into present-day Texas, there is evidence neither to confirm nor deny it. All that is known is that some adventurous Jews on horseback from the colony of Panuco rode north at the end of the sixteenth century, settled in Monclova, set up a cattle ranch, and then vanished from known history.

"Brave, daring, high-spirited" men and women, the Mexican historian Alfonso Toro calls them, belonging to "the hidalgo class"—somewhat of a romantic view. And yet, these Jewish conquistadors did live by "force of arms" in much the same manner of any settler in Mexico of the day; they were scholarly soldiers and Hebraic horsemen. "They were half merchants and half men-at-arms, who conquered the Indians in order to despoil them of their goods and to enslave them, who developed mines, and founded cattle ranches," Toro writes.

On the coasts and the plains of northeast Mexico a new era had begun. And the cattle ranches of the Jewish conquistadors and cowboys in the expedition of don Carvajal were harbingers of a new way of life in what would become the America West. The "conquest of Nuevo Leon was the most successful ever undertaken by New Spain," Simpson writes; "it transformed that remote corner of the kingdom into an orderly and prosperous community."

In spite of or perhaps because of his success, Governor Carvajal was arrested by the Inquisition. He was accused of being a "secret Jew."

The secretary to the king, Antonio Perez, had himself been accused of being a Jew. He had fled from the court of Spain and gone into hiding. Philip II ordered an investigation to find proof of Perez's heresy, and the royal charter to don Carvajal was presented as evidence.

Carvajal was then charged with "observing the Law of Moses." His grandmother, his mother, his wife, his sister, and her entire family were "apostates of the Holy Catholic faith," said the Inquisitor, Dr. Lobo (Spanish for "wolf") Guerrero, and don Carvajal had been their "aider, abetter, harborer and concealer." If he did not confess it was recommended that he be "put to torture."

One of the reluctant conquistadoras who had refused to sail with him had been his wife, doña Guiomar de Ribera. She was "a Jewess, but never had revealed that fact to her husband." If don Carvajal was naive about his wife's religious faith, he could not have been as ignorant about his sister's. She had been given in marriage at the age of twelve to a devout Portuguese Jew, Rodriguez de Matos. And when tortured on the rack by the fourth turn of the wheels—"Naked, covered with blood, defeated, she kneeled on the floor" and confessed; she was a Jew, so was her sister, the Governor's wife, and all of her family.

I believe and adore the Law of Moses, and not Jesus Christ. Have mercy on me, for I have told you the whole truth. I die! Oh, I die!

On the wooden scaffolding of the Inquisition, with a burning green candle in his hands, don Carvajal denied the accusations. "They tell me that my mother died in the Jewish faith," he said. "If that is so then she is not my mother, nor I her son." Nonetheless, he was imprisoned. He died within the year.

His sister, Francisca de Carvajal, was burned at the stake on December 8, 1596, in Mexico City. So was his nephew and namesake, Luis de Carvajal and his two nieces, Lernor and Cataliva de Leon y de la Cueva. In all, nine Jews were burned alive, ten were burned in effigy, and twenty-five were imprisoned, some for life.

On the collapse of the Carvajal family fortunes the royal persecutor sold their palatial "haciendas containing mares, mules and other animals." But there is no record of what happened to their Indian slaves. Nor is there any mention of the mestizo children, half-Jewish and half-Indian, of the Carvajal men.

Not all of the Carvajals fell victim to the Inquisition at that time. Some not only escaped, but set out on a new expedition.

One of the Carvajals, Juan de Vitoria, joined the Onate expedition that brought the first Spanish settlers to Nueva Espana, New Mexico, in 1598, two years after the auto-da-fé of the Holy Inquisition. He was a soldier, an *alferez,* or ensign. But, in later years, he ironically became the Standard Bearer of the Office of the Holy Inquisition in Nueva Espana. Even so his wife was accused of heresy, of using "magic roots" like an Indian, but there is no record of what happened to her or to her three sons.

The Catholic church historian Father Angelico Chavez writes that the reasons were "obscure," but no one seemed to know what had happened to "the remnants of a once great family." In Santa Fe, New Mexico, there is now not a single Carvajal.

And yet, I do not believe the pioneering Jewish ranchers and horsemen could have vanished completely into history, as had the Jewish conquistador, Hernando Alonso, before them. They remain with us as ghostly ancestors of the founders of our western history.

No one heretofore has thought them significant

enough to write about in any serious way. But the influence of their style of living and beliefs cannot be ignored; their memory persists in many of the traits of western ranching and horsemanship. These Jews were the first to bring the *gineta* riding style, the high-horned Persian, now western saddle, the tossed lasso, and the Andalusian ancestors of the quarter horse into the deserts of the Southwest. And they did it in their particular and peculiar way —as Jewish ranchers.

One of the qualities that has characterized the rancher is his taciturn and laconic nature. It is a quality that suggests a sense of privacy, the manner of a man who is closemouthed about himself and who does not wish a public display of his thoughts. That is not a quality rooted in the flamboyant verbosity of the conquistadors. But may it not have originated with the early western ranchers who had to hide their beliefs and hide themselves, the *conversos,* the hidden Spanish Jews?

These ranchers, of necessity, had to be unobtrusive and low-keyed to hide from the Inquisition. And yet the influence of the diffidence and reticense of the Jewish ranchers on the modern lifestyle of the cowboy ethic is little known. The roots of the ranching mystique have been traced to every possible influence, in my opinion, but where they originated. Those Jewish conquistadors who

moved north and became ranchers may be the
historical missing link that illuminates the coming of
the dark and dashing horsemen to America.

That may well be the most significant and
influential contribution of the Jewish conquistadors;
for whatever is consciously suppressed and hidden
can never be forgotten; it becomes a powerful and
eternal unconscious force no matter what disguises
and distortions clothe it.

⑨ The Don Quixotes of the New World

On their famed war stallions with banners flying and flags proudly held high, the would-be knights of the New World paraded into the plaza of Mexico City with their rusty armor creaking, some pieces missing, helmets dented and codpieces lost, celebrating their conquest. Inside the armor the men breathed heavily and sweated profusely in the semi-tropical heat. The sweat ran down their legs into their iron boots.

These self-proclaimed knights of the new aristocracy of the Americas nonetheless paraded with as much dignity as they could. For they were haughty men, surely the wealthiest, if not the most heroic conquerors that the world had seen since the Holy Crusades.

The enormous plaza of Mexico City had been designed specifically for their feudal tournaments and jousts. On the majestic square, before their great cathedral, the conquerors of the Aztec empire recreated the medieval splendor they had neither the money nor aristocratic traditions to enjoy in their rustic villages in Andalusia and Estremadura.

Now if the "Age of Chivalry" had died in Europe, it did not matter—they would revive it in America. The dream of Don Quixote became a reality in the Mexico of the conquistadors, where knighthood flowered once more and the pageantry of the gallant horsemen, resplendent in medieval adornments, reigned supreme. They had become *caballeros.*

In Spain, many of these newly ordained "gentlemen" had rarely ridden on a horse—they rode on mules. The old Spanish codes decreed that "gentlemen are implored by honor and tradition to ride on a horse; no gentleman shall ride on a mule," but few of these conquistadors had been gentlemen, back home.

Ferdinand, King of Spain, had ordered that any gentlemen found riding a mule would be punished; it was "effeminate" for a man to ride on an animal obviously meant for peasants and women. After all, the word for a gentleman was *caballero,* which meant a horseman.

And so when Columbus returned from his voyages, old and ill, and no longer able to mount a horse, he had to petition the king for special dispensation to ride a mule. The king, in 1505, issued a proclamation giving the admiral permission to retain his honor as a gentleman while sitting on a mule, something no other gentleman in the kingdom was permitted to do.

Even so, the gentlemen of Spain were prone to safer, slower mules than the willful horses that the Berbers and Bedouins had brought to the country. By 1634 the riding of mules had become so widespread that Prudencio de Sandoval in his book on Charles V, laments that the men of the land were becoming like "feeble women" because so many preferred mules to horses; he feared that the judgement of God was at hand, and the male potency of the nation was being dissipated by this cursed and "effeminate" practice that defamed the memories of knighthood and mocked the virility of manhood.

In the Americas such a fear was unfounded. The riding of horses became a symbol and test of manhood so widely accepted that by 1580 the nobleman Juan Garay wrote with disgust, "Even the beggars ride on horses." Any man could say he was a *caballero;* it was almost impossible to prove whether or not he was a descendant of the old nobility. "If a man rode like a knight, it was not wise to question his horse," was an old saying.

One of the most famous lords of the new knights was the Viceroy of Mexico, Luis de Velasco I, whose weekend tournaments rivaled those of the royal court. Every Saturday he would ride forth from his office in Mexico City to his country estates in Chapultepec with an entourage of eighty self-made aristocrats. In his gardens they would perform like the knights of old, feigning medieval tournaments as they jousted, charging one another on their galloping horses with long lances that broke upon their armor breastplates. And so the colonial officials became knights for a day. Almost but not quite—the lances these new knights so proudly held and faced so heroically were swamp reeds. . . .

And yet, not even that diminished the grandeur of their medieval games. In their imagination the lances they jousted with were fashioned of gold and silver, as surely as they were the new knights of Spain. They were the Don Quixotes of the New World.

Don Quixote, as Cervantes suggests, is really a conquistador. He is the common man as an aristocrat, whose nobility consists of his quest for his nonexistent nobility. This is fittingly expressed in his horse who is described as *tenetum pellis et ossa fuit,* nothing but skin and bones, and whose name, *Rocinante,* was from the word *rocin* that meant a nag, a hack horse, a swayback, whom the gentleman of La Mancha insists was "far better" than the horse of Alexander the Great, Bucephalus ("the Phallus of an Ox") or the horse of El Cid, Babieca. This nag, says Don Quixote, is "worthy of a knight."

Many of these less than aristocratic knights liked to boast that they were the sons of *hidalgos* (Spanish nobles). But most were "rustics who had left villages under a cloud, orphans and children who had left families incapable of supporting them," notes Francois Chevalie in *Land and Society in Colonial Mexico.* Few were of the noble birth they claimed and these were often from the declassed, or imaginary, aristocracy.

The Don Quixotes of his realm were "common people" said the Viceroy Velasco I in 1554: "Very few were *caballeros* or *hijosdalgo,*" the sons of gentlemen. They were *gente comun.*" And the Viceroy Marquez de Mancera, a century later, cynically wrote: "In these provinces, generally speaking, the *caballero* is a merchant and the merchant is a *caballero.* I see no objection to that, but rather a convenience from the political point of view"; it made the restless ex–horse-soldiers, the former conquistadors, content to believe in their own images of themselves.

Spanish philosopher Jose Ortega y Gasset was to say of these somewhat vainglorious men: "The tendency of the Andalusians to present and mimic themselves reveals a surprising collective narcissism." The Andalusian was the sort of man, he said, who "gives himself pleasure through his own form and being"; he was whatever he imagined himself to be.

But if the knighthood of the conquistadors was somewhat imaginary, their horses were real enough. From the beginning of their expeditions they realized the importance of their horses in their conquests. The horse more than anything else, became the source of their psychological power and their military might.

So many horses had been shipped to the New World during the conquest that the rulers of Spain ordered an embargo of the export of horses from the kingdom. By the middle of the sixteenth century, Antonio de Herrera notes that many of the conquistadors no longer lived by plunder but by raising horses. They had become, writes Matias de Motas, ranchers in spite of themselves. The riding of horses may not have made men into knights, but the horse was the vehicle of the empire.

On the second voyage of Columbus in 1493, a royal *cedula* commanded that he take along "twenty lancers with horses." These were the first horses that the Spaniards brought to the New World:

fifteen stallions and ten mares. And so successful were horses in battles with Indians that the following year Columbus wrote to the Queen of Spain: "Each time there is sent any type of boat there should be included some brood mares."

Even then, the admiral had the forboding that the horses sent for farming and breeding would be employed in gold-seeking and conquest. The horses ought not to be used in vainglorious pursuits, said Columbus, and her majesty ought to regulate their export and use.

And so, on his third voyage to the New World in 1498, Columbus was requested by the Emperor to take along "forty *jinetes*," horsemen and horses, the finest in Spain who rode in the Berber style. But in the mercenary spirit of the time, the *jinetes* sold the Emperor's horses, bought ordinary "nags" in their stead, and pocketed the money.

The casual and callous way in which the conquistadors treated their horses was evident in how they shipped them to the Americas. On the small galleons the horses were kept on the deck in the scorching sun. They were suspended in slings, in the air, and they bobbed and swayed with each wave. If the galleons were larger, the horses were kept between decks, in the darkness, and suspended in that same strange way. The long voyages of two or three months were extremely hard on the poor imprisoned animals, and more than half of them died during the ocean crossings.

So many carcasses of dead horses were fed to the sea on the route to the New World that it came to be known as the "Horse Latitudes." When horses died, or if ship rations were low, the horses were thrown overboard.

If these starved and abused horses survived their cruel voyage and were landed safely in the Americas, their troubles had just begun. The moist and dense tropical climate was difficult to adjust to. Horses died in large numbers.

Nor did the conquistadors' practice of the belief that they were medieval knights rest easily on the beleaguered animals. The armor of steel and silver-ornamented saddles, some weighing hundreds of pounds, that the Spaniards saddled their horses with were a severe burden in the tropical sun. Many horses went beserk. There were repeated accounts of maddened horses charging wildly into armies of Indians, biting warriors in frenzied fear, and being shot to death with arrows. Cortez had lost his personal mount in this way.

The conquistadors use of horses in battle was pedestrian. It had little of the vivacious style of the Moslem horsemen, and none of the tactical brilliance of the Mongols; they deployed their horses in no original and unique formations, and they employed them not as a trained cavalry, but individually. Each rider rode *a la gineta,* as he wished. If anything, the conquistadors were a cavalry of individualists. Little evidence can be found of any prearranged battle plans or strategy. And the *gineta* style of riding they had learned from the Berbers was perfect for the feats of individual daring that they loved and so well suited the Spanish temperament.

Fra Bernal Diaz, the chronicler of the Cortez expedition, writes: "The Conquest was made *a la gineta.*" But he did not say why.

The comment of the conquistador don Pedro de Casteneda de Nagera was perhaps nearer the truth. "In the new country horses are the most necessary things," he said, "for they frighten the enemy the most, and after God, we owed our victory to our horses." It was not the conquistadors' horsemanship, but their horses, that defeated the Indians; for the Indians never expressed the awe and fear of the conquistadors themselves that they expressed about their horses.

Not that the Indians necessarily thought that these horses were four-legged men or the monstrous gods that the Spaniards thought that they thought they were. If they had, they would not have learned to ride horses so fast and so well. Rather, it may have been that the Indians simply had no military weapons that provided the mobility and power that horses gave the invaders. For want of a horse, more than for any other reason, it may be said, their empire fell.

Even the land given to the conquistadors as spoils of war was determined by their horsemanship. If a man was merely a foot soldier, a *peon,* he was given a small parcel called a *peonia;* but if he was a *caballero,* a horseman, he was given a *caballeria,* five times the amount of land in a *peonia.*

In the days of feudal knighthood a *caballeria* was the war booty that a knight received after battle. It could be gold, or a woman, or land, whatever—the *caballeria* was the knight's share. And the word ironically became synonymous with chivalry, a less romantic idea in feudal times than later. But in Mexico the old meaning of the word was revived; it meant the spoils of battle, not nobility as we like to think of it.

In the medieval tales of heroism that the conquistadors liked to tell of their exploits, it was often their horses, not themselves, who were the heroes. And so it was in the romantic tale told of Panfilo de Narvaez, a "well born gentleman," who was sent to conquer western Cuba. Of all his men, he alone had a horse. Encamped one night in a tropical forest, his small force of Spaniards was attacked by what seemed to be "seven thousand Indians." The gentleman horseman, awakened from his sleep, leaped naked onto his horse wearing only his white shirt, and with bells tied to the tail of his mare he rode through the startled Indians.

So frightened by this specter of a naked conquistador on horseback were the Indians, says de Narvaez, that they fled in haste. "Neither man, woman or child stopped running," he reports, until they had reached Camaquey—two hundred miles away.

One of the commoner sports of the conquistadors, knowing the symbolic power of their horses, was to use them to taunt and intimidate the Indians. They did so with a bravado that may have delighted them more than it frightened the Indians.

In Peru there was such a time when Pizarro had sent the impetuous young Hernando DeSoto with a message to the Emperor of the Incas, Atahualpa, who in politeness ordered a body of soldiers to welcome his visitor. "On seeing them," says a contemporary account, "DeSoto, to let them know that if they were not his friends, he alone was quite sufficient to battle all of them, charged his horse at full gallop and halted close to the Inca." So close did he come, says another account, that his horse snorted in the face of the Emperor. And then, belatedly remembering where he was, the young man dismounted and bowed courteously. The cowboy-like bit of rodeo riding did not alarm the Emperor, who, it is said, "did not bat an eyelash."

In such horse showmanship Cortez was more successful. On landing at the River of Grijalva in the Yucatan, he ordered that the *Caciques* of the local tribes submit to him in peace and contrived to trick them into submission with his horses. Cortez told his soldiers: "Do you know, gentlemen, it appears to me these Indians have a great fear of our horses. They really believe they are the ones who make war on them." And he took the stallion of his musician, Ortiz, a *"muy rijoso,"* a lusty horse, and had him scent a mare who had just foaled, but then ordered them separated. As the *Caciques* came and seated themselves for the council, Cortez had the mare and stallion brought and tied on either side of the nervous peace conference.

"Scenting the mare [the stallion] began to paw the ground and roll his eyes and neigh, wild with excitement," writes an eyewitness. "The *Caciques*, thinking he was roaring at them, were petrified with fear." Cortez, seeing that "the ruse had worked, informed the Indians that he had told the horses not to harm them since they had come for peace."

No wonder that in the mourning of their dead after a battle, the conquistadors grieved as much for their horses as their men. In his lamentation after the *noche triste* when the Aztecs had nearly annihilated his army, Cortez said, "It was the greatest grief to think upon the horses, and the valiant men, we had lost."

And similarly DeSoto, explorer of what is now part of the United States, after his defeat at the Cherokee village he called Mauvilla, where he had lost eighty soldiers, proclaimed that the "five and forty [dead] horses were no less mourned than were the men, for in them [the horses] is the greatest strength of the army." Though DeSoto added that he mourned his horses "after the Christians," that seems to have been an obligatory afterthought.

Conquistadors may not have been the horsemen they imagined they were, but they knew their horses were their most valuable asset. That may be seen in the esteem with which Bernal Diaz lists the horses of the Cortez expedition; he writes of them in more loving detail and at as great length as he does the men. Each horse is fondly described by name, color, and characteristics. It provoked the historian William Prescott into remarking that Diaz's list was "minute enough for the pages of a sporting calendar."

The mount of the conquistador was more than an animal he rode—it was the measure of the man.

And the man was judged by how well he rode, with what daring and with what style; the style was most important.

And so the medieval tournaments of the conquistadors evolved through the years into spectacular displays of horsemanship. These rituals were like modern-day rodeos in that they pitted men against wild horses and bulls as once knight had faced knight in deadly games where the prize was wealth and glory and defeat often meant death. No Mexican fiesta of the conquistadors was complete without its equestrian feats and pseudo-jousts, although these exhibits of horsemanship became progressively less courtly than cruel, less ritual than real, less European than American.

In the earliest bullfight, for example, the aim was to ride the bull *a jaripeo,* to death, or to cut its muscles with *desjarretaferas,* bullhooks, or simply to kill the bull by shooting it. One account tells of such a bullfight that took place at the Santisima Trinidad hacienda in 1620, when the Bishop Mota y Escobar came visiting. The lord of the hacienda sent a "large body of horsemen" to greet His Eminence by performing feats of horsemanship that left the Bishop "with mouth agape" at their defiance of death. Not to be outdone, the Bishop entered the bullfight that followed to demonstrate his own manly skills. He killed the bull with a single, well-aimed shot.

The horse and rider faced the wild bull as they would face an enemy in battle. One way or another the rider had to conquer his enemy, even if he had to kill him, to show his manhood.

In modern Mexico the *Charreada,* the Fete of the Charros, is based upon these ancient Mexican tournaments of the conquistadors. The charro was more than a *vaquero,* a cowboy; he was a feudal knight dressed in cowboy clothes, resplendent in finery, who performed the feats of chivalry in an American style, but with the spirit of European knighthood. Even after four centuries the ideas of manhood that govern the equestrian feats have changed hardly at all. And many of the old tests of knightly manhood are still performed.

One of these is the *Paso de la Muerte,* the Pass of Death. In this event the charro places his saddle in the middle of the arena and mounts his horse bareback. A wild mare is brought and the charro gives chase. He grasps the wild mare with his right hand, at full gallop, jumps from his horse onto the wild one, rides it until it begins to buck, and then jumps off, landing on his feet. If the charro loses his hat he is disqualified. He has to try to retain his dignity.

And then there is the *Jinete de Novillos,* the

Riding of the Bull, named for the old Berber way of riding *a la gineta*. In this event, after catching the bull by the tail and tossing it to the ground, the charro mounts the bull and rides it not for eight seconds as in a rodeo, but until the bull becomes calmed and the man becomes its master.

These rituals grew from the old Spanish colonial rule when only Spaniards were permitted to ride on horses, "in an attempt to control the Indian peasants," says Rolando Romero, the Master Charro of the recent Charreada held in Santa Fe, New Mexico. "As the ranches grew, more help was needed, however, and the mixed Spanish/Indian classes [the *mestizos*] were trained in horsemanship which they brought to a high art."

Yet "being a charro is more than being a cowboy," he says. "There's a sense of honor and bearing that goes with the title." For the charro must always be ready "to defend a lady in distress."

"A charro is more than a cowboy," says Romero. "He is a gentleman."

10   *Blessed Souls in Purgatory: The Cowboys*

The first cowboy, or *vaquero,* in Mexico may have been a Moorish slave. In the royal documents of Mexico the earliest man listed by the title of *vaquero* was a nameless black slave of Cortez, who in the census of 1549 on a slave farm of the conqueror, that of Atelina in the present-day province of Morelos, was listed simply as "the *vaquero*"; he was a *Morisco,* a half-Moor.

Black *vaqueros* were common on the early ranches of Mexico. The Indians were not permitted to ride horses; they might all too easily escape to their villages. That was not possible for Africans or *Moriscos.*

And so, in the sixteenth century, the first *vaqueros* were most often "mestizos, mulattos and free Negroes," says an early document on ranching. The conquistadors might have been *caballeros,* gentlemen on horseback, but they were not often *hombres de caballos,* men of the horses; they loved to ride them and often had estates that raised them, but they did not work them.

In the Archives of the Indies there is mention of one *vaquero* earlier than the nameless Moor, but his existence is shadowy. On the passenger list of the expedition of Diego Garcia that set sail from Seville in 1513 there was a shepherd, Alonso Martin of Andalusia, and a fruit farmer, Alonso de Andujar, a *Morisco,* and Sebastian de Mendoza, who seems to have been a *converso* or converted Jew and who was listed as a *"vaquero."* But, there is no evidence of Mendoza ever working as a cowboy in the New World. If he did, he would have had to have done so in the Indies, for Mexico had not yet been invaded.

Not that it mattered. Whether the first *vaquero* was a Moor, a black African, a Jew, or an Andalusian peasant, the style of horsemanship he brought to the Americas had its origins in Africa and Asia. The early *vaqueros* were rarely Spanish gentlemen.

Ranching and farming were not among the

favored occupations of the conquistadors. If they did reluctantly set up an *estancia,* a farm, or a *ranchero,* a ranch, they seldom worked on it. They were knights and any manual labor was an insult. So the ranch hands and *vaqueros* were almost always African and Indian slaves. When slavery was prohibited those who stayed on the ranches to work for wages were the second-generation mestizos and mulattos, the half-Indian and half-African children of the conquistadors, the absentee landlords.

So few of these conquistadors lived on their farms that in the Archbishopric of Mexico City in 1596, the one hundred fifty *estancias* surrounding the capital had barely two hundred Spaniards in residence. And yet the census showed eight thousand farmers and ranchers living in Mexico City.

The raising of cattle and horses was left to the mestizos and mulattos. Later, when they too had mastered the horse, the Indians were to become the *vaqueros.* And it was these men, not the Spaniards, who were the ranch managers, ranch hands, and cowboys. Curiously, when the conquistadors who made their fortunes in ranching returned with their new-found riches they were disparagingly called *"Indianos."*

No Indian had been permitted to ride, much less own, a horse until the enlightened Viceroy

Velasco, recognizing the need for Indian *vaqueros,* rescinded the royal prohibition. By 1555 the former Indian slaves were encouraged to become skilled horsemen and horse breeders. And they were given permission to own pack horses. One thing was forbidden them—they were not allowed to own a saddle. And so, the Indian *vaqueros* rode bareback, with nothing more than a halter, a restriction that actually helped make them better rather than worse riders.

The saddle, as much as the horse, was a symbol of knighthood of the New World Spaniards. In Spain, since the conquistadors weren't true gentlemen, they had ridden mules and donkeys without a saddle, feet dangling, with neither stirrups nor spurs, as befitted the peasantry. Gentlemen alone had saddles. So when they became *caballeros* in Mexico, the saddle became the symbol of status and they fashioned the most ornate and elaborate saddles, adorned with silver and beautifully tooled leather. A man's saddle was a sign of his wealth and his esteem, and the Indians were now the saddless peasants.

Even so, on one of the first cattle ranches in Mexico, founded by Jeronimo Lopez in 1521, almost all the *vaqueros* were Indians. And when Governor Diego de Ibarra of Viscaya established his pioneering ranches in northern Mexico, near

Zacatecas, he hired Indian *vaqueros* almost exclusively. These tribal cowboys ran a ranch so vast that its great herds of cattle numbered a hundred and thirty thousand head. And its herds of horses covered entire valleys. By 1650 the ranches of Sonora and Chihuahua, where the *vaqueros* were wholly local Indians, were said to be stocked with five hundred thousand cows.

On these cattle ranches the herds grew so large so fast, that in a few generations they spread over the land "like the waves of the rising tide," said one observer. "Cattle are being born and multiplying unbelievably," said the Viceroy Velasco. "You cannot exaggerate or imagine the spectacle that is before your eyes." In the Toluca Valley alone, where cattle were introduced in 1535, by 1555 there were a hundred and fifty thousand head. There were single ranches with twenty thousand, fifty thousand, and a hundred thousand head. And on the grassy valleys of the north the flocks of sheep were even larger; in Queretaro in 1579 there were two hundred thousand sheep and in Nuevo Leon in 1650 there were three hundred thousand.

And on the rangelands of the mountain plateaus the herds of horses multiplied as profusely. In the small town of San Juan del Rio there were ten thousand saddle horses and in the tiny native village of Tacuba there were three thousand pack horses. So many horses were bred by the *vaqueros* that the saying was: "Even the humblest mestizo and the poorest Spaniard possesses his own horses." Still, the rancher conquistadors complained about the Indian *vaqueros*. They were idlers. They were nomads. If an Indian did not like the work on a ranch he got on his horse and rode off. They wandered across the land as though it still belonged to them. They were *ferarum,* "wild animals."

These Indian *vaqueros* lived off the land by rustling horses and cattle. The art of stealing horses, in their hands, became a skilled profession. Even worse, said the perplexed Viceroy Velasco, they committed "murder, theft and other excesses"; he suggested they be "civilized" by settling them in cities, but he believed they were too stubborn and independent-willed to be persuaded to give up their freedom.

Spaniards who became *vaqueros* learned from these Indians. They too were young, bold, and restless men. They were "like corks floating on the water," wrote Father Antonio Tello. And Martin Cortez, son of the conqueror, complained in 1536 that it was difficult to govern a population that consisted of "an infinite number of wanderers" who lived largely by the "rustling of cattle"; while the Viceroy Velasco II petitioned the Emperor to halt emigration to the Americas because the population consisted "mostly [of] wanderers, whence arises great disorder and confusion" in the land.

The once glorious soldiers had no more great wars to fight. If some new expedition was proclaimed, hundreds rushed to join it. When Coronado announced that he was marching to the north to seek the fabled, but unfortunately nonexistent Seven Cities of Cibola, they "were on the verge of depopulating Mexico City," wrote Suarez de Peralta. In the cities they felt confined and frustrated; they were bored. And they fled into the countryside.

On the ranches and *estancias* these young men came to lead a vagabond's life. They wandered from one hacienda to another. In time people began calling them "saddletree boys," *hijos de fuste,* said a royal magistrate in 1607, "because their sole possessions are a wretched old saddle, a lightly stepping mare [that was stolen], and their gun or short lance." So the image of the man who lives in his saddle was born.

"They called themselves *vaqueros.* They ride about armed with a knife. They collect in bands and no one dares withstand them," wrote a royal inspector. "They strike terror in the heart of the population."

And yet, men who were skilled as horsemen

were so few that hiring "mounted brigands as cowboys" became a common practice. Then, as now, the men would drift off after roundup time when the *rodeos* were ended. But the ranchers had little choice but to hire them, for there were no others to do *vaquero* work. In Zacatecas ranchers had a saying, "Their presence is an evil, but their absence is a much greater one."

In many ways the Mexican *vaqueros* developed the traits that later were to be thought typical of the western cowboy. The wanderlust, the sense of independence and "movin' on," the stubborn pride, the free spirit, and the delight in daring horsemanship all were to become characteristic of the American West; but all these things were originally Mexican.

"The Mexican cowboy's influence was so widespread," writes historian Francois Chevalier, "that it impressed his American counterpart in the last century, who took over his rodeo, saddle, stirrups [Andalusian in origin], huge spurs, apparel, and even, in all likelihood, character traits."

On the rugged terrain of the northern frontier of Mexico with its labyrinths of canyons and caves, the Mexican Indians who had become *vaqueros* were in their natural element. They were at home. In these lands, so foreign and in hospitable to the Spaniards, they were comfortable and native. So, they combined their newly acquired skills as horsemen with their old knowledge of the country.

As the great herds were driven farther and farther to the north, the land became more and more primeval and formidable. The land with its lofty mountains and cruel deserts shaped everything upon it. Even the free-riding spirit of the *vaqueros* was reshaped by the necessities of the harsh, barren expanses of the Great American Desert that stretched from Texas to California, from Sonora and Chihuahua north to Montana.

In the intense and unrelenting heat of the Southwest sun the *vaqueros* developed the trappings that became known as "cowboy" or "western." There was a wide brimmed hat, a *sombrero,* that became the ever present cowboy symbol, worn in the bath if not also in bed. There were the leggings, or *botas,* that protected the cowboy's legs from the cactus, later replaced by the *chappareras* or chaps. There was the small, open *chaqueta,* or jacket, a garment later immortalized by Levi Strauss.

The riding gear of the *vaqueros* was equally and uniquely "Americanized" by the terrain. From their Persian and Berber crested saddles they developed the high-horned western saddles needed for roping wild and near-wild range cattle. And for roping at full gallop they lengthened the old, short lassos that had been handed down from the Persians until they became the long lariats, *las reatas,* of today.

On the lonely and long rides across the desert, over distances unknown in Europe, the *vaqueros* had to carry many supplies. So they hung a array of saddlebags on their horses, the *coginillos,* that forced the elimination of the ornate decorations that the conquistadors so loved. Instead of these feudal affectations they developed the use of a saddleblanket, a *sarape saltillo,* that served as a *poncho* and as a bedroll on cold desert nights.

And most important, they bred horses whose ancestors had been the Berber *barbs* and the Puerto Rican *paso finos* and whose descendants became the mustangs and quarter horses of the West. Tough and resilient, these horses were bred to the terrain. For the men and their animals both had to learn to adapt themselves to a way of living and to a way of thinking that was new and strange to them.

On the grassy plains of eastern New Mexico, the "staked plains," one of the first cattle roundups in the West illustrates that sometimes difficult process of adaptation. It happened in 1598 during the settlement of the territory by the expedition of don Juan de Onate. His settlers had run out of meat and Onate ordered his lieutenant, Vicente Zaldivar, to take some men and hunt for wild game. Near the present border of Texas the hunting party came upon "a hundred thousand wild cattle." Wild buffalo! From their experience in rounding up the half-wild longhorns of Andalusia they built a corral, with a V-shaped fence leading into it and attempted to drive the buffalo into it. But the startled buffalo would not cooperate. "They are terrible obstinate cattle," said Zaldivar, and "courageous beyond exaggeration."

Being unable to corral these "wild cattle," the *vaqueros* deciced to lasso their calves. They roped them easily enough, but then discovered that they could not force the calves to leave their mothers. And so the first cattle roundup turned out to be something less than a success, though it did introduce these "wild cattle" to the no less "wild" *vaqueros,* and the *cibolero,* or buffalo hunter, was born.

For the *vaqueros* were not the sequined and bespangled *charros* of myth, riding through the cactus with singing guitars. They were men from the dry, hard, merciless earth of the unforgiving deserts of several continents. In them was created a unique blend of different styles of horsemanship that eventually came to be called American.

"The blood of *caballeros,* bullfighters, Jews, Moors, Basques and Indian heroes ran in the *vaquero*'s veins," writes the oldtime *vaquero* Arnold

R. Rojas in *The Vaquero.* "He was a strange mixture of races."

In remembering the earthy and bloody history of the *vaqueros,* Rojas writes of them and of his own family memory:

I have not come from an 'Old Spanish family.' Old Spanish families are the invention of the *gringos.* They are a myth which the *paisanos* have come to believe themselves, like Sancho did his enchantment with Dulcinea in *Don Quixote. . . .* The *Californiano* writer on California to the contrary called himself a *Sonoreno.* I have heard third and fourth generation descendants of the De Anza expedition say: *Nosotros somos Sonorenos. Sonora es nuestra tierra*—We are Sonorans. Sonora is our motherland.

And Rojas concludes about the *vaquero:*

He admired his Iberian father, but sided and sympathized with his raped Indian mother. If food was short he fed his horse before he fed his wife. Though often a strange contradiction he was, without doubt, the most interesting man in the New World.

In 1727, when the great cattle rancher, the Count of Miraville, asked the blessings and protections of the Saints for his hacienda and his horses, he evoked the dual spirit of the *vaqueros:*

noble and evil, full of reality and illusion, devoted to life but doomed.

He prayed:

First, St. Joseph as administrator of the hacienda.
Second, St. Anthony of Padua as Sheriff.
Third, the Venerable Don Juan de Palafox as Corporal.
Fourth, St. John of Nepomun as Adjutant.
Fifth, the Blessed Souls in Purgatory as Cowboys.

11 The Rise of the New Horse Nation

On the great prairies and in the high mountains of the southwestern territories of the United States the oldtime cowhands said that the Indians were the very best *vaqueros*. Arnold Rojas, one of the last of the *caballeros* of California, remembers them:

When a *vaquero* was especially skilled and he was asked how he reached such a degree of proficiency, his answer invariably would be *Me crie entre los Indios*—I was raised among the Indians.

Rancheros, the ranchers of the old Spanish and Mexican grants, used Indian *vaqueros* almost exclusively, until the Gold Rush period. The *vaquero,* or buckaroo, who herded cattle on the ranches of California was sometimes a Cahilla [Indian], a Piute, a Mission Indian or a member of the numerous tribes which populated California.

"A man took pride in calling himself *Indio*," Rojas says, for he had ridden with them in the old days, and he recalled that one "took more pride in calling himself *Indio* than in anything else. When some *vaquero* had performed with great skill, the other men would look at each other, smile approvingly, and say *Se crio entre los Indios*—Well, he was raised among the Indians."

The oldtime *vaquero* spoke of these Indians with awe in his voice. "Of the man who showed much 'Indian blood' in his makeup," he once said enviously, *"ese no le debe no los Buenas Dias a los Españoles*—that one doesn't owe even a Good Day to the Spaniards."

On the earlier ranches of the West the Indians were often the first cowhands. Their horsemanship was legendary.

It is thought that the Indians were "natural" horsemen. Surely this is a romantic idea, for these tribes of North America had never known of horses before the coming of the Spaniards. And so their horsemanship was a newly acquired skill that rapidly became an old tribal tradition; it was somewhat like the common belief that Indians were "born in the saddle," when in truth few Indians had saddles.

Still, the nomadic Indian tribes of the West "took to the horse" with an enthusiasm and expertise that seemed uncanny. They rode with an ease that was amazing. Not only did they ride bareback, but they rode with an equal skill on the horse's neck, his shank, his side, and even underneath, with their legs hooked on his back, so that whites who observed the Indians' acrobatic feats would say in the popular saying of the day: "The Indian rides as though he was part of his horse."

The riding of the Indian was wonderful to some, but it was unnerving to others. It seemed supernatural and mysterious, even diabolical, that they rode so well though horses were new to them.

And yet the attitude of most Indians toward their horses was not at all mystical. They looked on the horse as an animal that was useful and pleasurable to ride. Few of the tribes ever deified the horse as so many civilizations had. Nor did they treat the horse as though it was the measure of a man, the symbol of their manhood, or test of their virility as the Spaniards did.

The horse was a horse. Nothing more than an animal of strength that brought a measure of wealth and fortunately happened to have come to them on their path through life. It was to be used, not worshipped, and when a horse was no longer of any use it was abandoned.

Some of those same whites who thought the

Indians were natural horsemen thought that their treatment of their horses was unnatural. They did not groom them. They abused them. They rode them to death. And worst of all they ate them.

Many of these Indian horses, in the beginning, were of the finest breeds of Andalusia. They had been brought to the western territories by the "equestrian priests and monks" of the Franciscan and Jesuit orders. And these "monks' horses" and "missionary horses" were made available to the Indians in defiance of royal prohibition because the fathers needed *vaqueros* for their herds at the early missions.

Perhaps the finest horses in the West were those of the Carthusian monks. These steeds were the descendants of the *Garanomes Guzmanes* and *Valenzuela* horses of Andalusia, who were bred from the Berber stock commemorated to this day in the majestic statues of rearing stallions on the boulevard of Jerez.

"Equestrian monks who came to the New World," says Rojas, "taught the ancient Hispano-Arabic hippology" to the Indians. The horsemanship of the monks was one of the *cosas de muy lejos atras,* the things of the distant past, they had learned from the Moors of North Africa. And so the heathens of America were taught African heathens' arts by the good padres of Catholic Spain.

Of all the padres none was as influential in bringing horsemanship to North America as Father Kino—his missions in Sonora and Arizona bred as many horses and cattle as they did converts. Had he not been a priest, Father Kino may have been remembered as a cattle baron. And his *vaqueros* at Mission Dolores and San Xavier del Bac near Tucson were nearly all native Indians. There was hardly a Spaniard amongst them. The purpose of his evangelical mission was to baptize the "pagans," but he treated them humanely and gave them horses.

Sonoran tribes like the Opata, Seri, Mayo, and Yaqui began using horses by the late 1600s. They worked on the ranches and drove the packhorses in the mines of the conquistadors and on the missions. And these horses, too, spread northward into the unexplored lands of New Spain.

On those stark deserts and unconquered mountains to the north, fear and awe of the land seemed to possess the Spaniards. They felt isolated and often lost in the expanse of land as vast as the sky. And since they were uneasy and unsure of themselves they became suspicious and fearful of the people whom they could not conquer as they had those of Mexico.

No people in all of the Americas fought longer and more successfully against the Spaniards than did the Commanches and Apaches. And no rebellion was as disasterous to the Spaniards as the Revolt of the Pueblo Indians of New Mexico in 1680, when the defeated conquistadors had to abandon the entire territory. The sight of mounted Indians began to terrify them and, unlike the missionaries, they desperately attempted to keep horses out of Indian hands.

Even so the Apaches and Commanches had horses by the late 1590s and became expert horsemen. When the "Founder of New Mexico," don Juan de Onate, crossed the Rio Grande in 1597, he was met by mounted Apache riders whom he christened the *Vaquero* tribe, the "Cowboy Tribe." For nearly a century afterward these people were known to the Spaniards not as Apaches, but as *Vaqueros.* In the same way the Spaniards called the Commanches the "Horse Indians." And so the word *vaquero* became synonymous with the Indians.

Nowadays the word *vaquero* conjures up a romantic figure of the western knight errant. But in that time the Spaniards used the word as a curse; it was no honor to compare a man with an Indian, because the *vaquero* (Indian) was the figure of fear —he was hated and he was dangerous.

Of all the tribes of horsemen none impressed the Spaniards as much as the Commanches. "They are so skilled in horsemanship that they have no equal," writes de Mezieres, a royal official, in 1770. Their horses are "as numerous as the stars," he declares, and "as beautiful."

The Commanche horses made the Spaniards so envious that they stole them in large numbers. On one raid in 1777, the Governor of New Mexico, de Anza, boasted that his troops had stolen "more than five hundred horses" from the camps of the Commanches. And the Indians, not to be outdone, retaliated by raiding the Spanish ranches and villages and stealing about two thousand horses in return.

On the Great Plains farther to the north, the explorers and traders from the East were equally envious of the Indian horsemen. Coming upon some Cheyenne horses near the Missouri River in 1806, a traveler, Alexander Henry, called them "beautiful spirited animals." They were "by far the best built and most active horses in this country," he said. "Not so," said Zebulon Pike, for whom Pike's Peak is named. The "most beautiful" horses belonged to the Pawnees, who had "vast quantities of excellent horses" that were "far superior." While Lewis and Clark, on seeing the fabled Appaloosas of the Nez Percé, proclaimed that *they* were by far the most beautiful and as good as "our best blooded horses in Virginia."

And the mountain man Jim Bridger, believing

the Commanches had the best horses, rode one of theirs; while Kit Carson, who had a Commanche wife, rode a horse named "Apache," for the horses of the Apaches, he said, were unsurpassed by any others.

On his travels in the West in 1823, the phlegmatic Duke of Wurttemberg grumbled that such talk was romantic nonsense. The Indians' horses were ungroomed, unwashed, unshod, poorly fed if not starved, misshapen animals, he said. It was not their horses but their horsemen that made the Indians such "unbelievable" riders.

The tale was told of how upon a "miserable sheep of a pony" a Commanche raced and defeated the finest of U.S. Army stallions. It happened at Fort Chadbourne in Texas, where the Commanche defeated all opponents in three races, then in the fourth added insult to defeat by riding backwards on his horse and making "hideous grimaces" to the U.S. cavalry riders who trailed behind him. Although his horse was no more than an "American dog," says Frank Dobie, the horsemanship of the Indian was incredible.

The men of the U.S. cavalry wanted the Indians' horses as badly as had the soldiers of Spain. And so they stole them as freely. In 1874, the troops of General MacKenzie captured more than a thousand horses from the Commanches and Kiowas and, after taking the finest for themselves, slaughtered the entire herd in the Tule Canyon of the Texas panhandle. There was a "great collection of whitened bones" of horses stolen from the Indians stored there. The cavalry justified the rustling and killing of Indian horses on the grounds that they were weakening the fighting ability of the tribes; the theft of a horse from them was a patriotic act.

And so when the Kiowa surrendered at Fort Sill, after the fight in the Palo Duro Canyon the first thing the U.S. cavalry did was to kill the horses. In a field they slaughtered eight hundred horses at once. Then "two thousand more were sold, stolen, or given away."

On the northern plains theft of Indian horses was encouraged for the same reasons. In 1876, the U.S. cavalry stole nearly three thousand horses from the Cheyenne and Sioux. Then, they drove the herd into a blizzard until almost all of them had died. It is difficult to say if that was a vengeful act or a military tactic.

If the soldiers stole horses from the Indians as the Indians did from the soldiers, the mountain men stole from everyone. One of the daring members of that nefarious breed, Jim Beckwourth, boasted he personally had stolen eighteen hundred horses from the *rancheros* of California. And Pegleg Smith, enboldened by good amounts of "Taos lightning," raided the herds of soldiers and Indians alike in Texas, but made off with "only about three thousand head"—which he sold to the gentlemen horsemen of the East. The mountain man Bill Williams, in an even more daring exploit, attempted to drive a herd of fifteen hundred stolen horses and mules from California to New Mexico; he lost most of them on the way. Rufus Sage, with a band of twenty-two mountain men, claimed to have stolen more than three thousand horses and lost half of them.

One of the most adventurous of these horse thieves was a Dane, Daniel Bruhn, who in 1871 joined "a bandit crew such as would be difficult to find the like in Europe," he enthused. They stole three thousand horses in California and foolheartedly attempted to drive them over the Sierra Nevada, a disasterous mistake. After six months on the trail, Bruhn gave up the rustler's life and returned to Denmark where he became the director of the Royal Academy of Fine Arts.

None of the rustling and horse thievery of the Indians equalled the grand larceny of horseflesh committed by the mountain men and the U.S. Cavalry. The Indians were amateurs by comparison. But, as usual, the Indians were accused of the crimes committed against them, and they were blamed for the successes of the white men.

Even today, a popular belief persists that the Indians acquired most of their horses either by capturing wild mustangs or by stealing them from others. Neither is entirely true. On the early frontier fewer horses wandered free than is imagined. Horses were precious to the pioneers and so were carefully guarded, for without horses soldiers and settlers might not survive.

And as to theft—the Indians stole horses as acts of courage and manhood. They did not steal horses in huge herds as the white rustlers did, to sell for profit in the eastern cities.

Most of the horses that the Indians had they got unromantically by trading for them. Commanches and Apaches were particularly good horse traders. They had appeared at the great trade fairs at Taos and Pecos since the days of the conquistadors, offering medicine and captives for horses and weapons. The King of Spain ordered that horses be traded for Indian captives, in the name of Christianity; if it was necessary to trade horses for Indians to save their souls, a royal decree demanded that it be done.

At one trade fair in New Mexico in 1699, the Spaniards wrote of Navajos who offered goodly amounts of French carbines and cannon, shoes, jewels, waistcoats, sword belts, and Pawnee women and children. They demanded horses in return.

Spanish horses became an important trade commodity between different tribes as well. In 1680, when the French explorer Robert Cavelier de La Salle reached Illinois, he noted that the local tribes had horses they had obtained in trade with the Apaches, one thousand miles away. And when the French missionaries explored the Upper Missouri they discovered these horses as far north as the Canadian border.

On the Missouri River in 1739, where the French explorer Vérendrye visited the Mandan villages, he found "several tribes that use horses and carry on trade." These mounted Indians traded furs and skins for corn and beans, Vérendrye says; he called them "People of the Horses."

For many of the Indian people the horse and the men who brought it caused the most powerful changes in their lives. If they were a hunting people it increased their range and made them swifter than their prey, for the horse was a hunting machine of advanced technology to a people whose only domesticated animals were dogs. Some say the horse brought about the Golden Age of the tribes.

And yet, the horse to the Indians was neither god nor demon. It was an animal of great strength and wonder, but it was an animal and as such part of nature as they were.

So the Navajos sang of their horses in the Horse Song:

My horse has a hoof like a striped agate,
his fetlock is like a fine eagle plume,
his legs are like lightning.

My horse's body is like an arrow of eagle feathers.

My horse has a tail like a thin black cloud.

The Holy Wind blows through his mane, his mane is
made of rainbows.

My horse's ears are made of round corn.

My horse's eyes are made of stars.

I am wealthy because of him.
I am eternal and peaceful.
I stand for my horse.

To the Indian, the horse never assumed the
mythic power of other animals, such as the coyote,
or the bear, or the owl. He remained nothing more
than a horse.

So the singers sang:

Before me peaceful.
Behind me peaceful.
Beneath me peaceful.
Above me peaceful.
Around me peaceful.

Peaceful am I when my horse neighs.

On the stormy plains the horse was seen as less
peaceful; it was angry as the winds. There too the

horse was part of nature; it was made from the dry earth according to the Kiowa tale.

The story of how the Kiowa had created the horse was remembered by Scott Momaday in *The Way to the Rainy Mountain:*

Long ago the Kiowa decided to make a horse; they decided to make it out of clay, and so they began to shape the clay with their hands. Well, the horse began to be. But it was a terrible, terrible thing. It began to writhe, slowly at first, then faster and faster until there was a great commotion everywhere. The wind grew up and carried everything away. Even now, when they see the storm clouds gathering, the Kiowas know what it is: that a strange animal roams the sky. It has the head of a horse . . .

The "lightning comes from the mouth, and the tail, whipping and thrashing on the air, makes the high, hot wind of the tornado," they say.

Riding the horse-tornado, the *Man-ka-hi,* "they are not afraid," they say. The horse is a natural element. It is part of human life. And that is how one rides it.

Not having saddles and often not wanting them, the Indian horsemen learned to ride bareback. They moved in unison with the rhythm, the gait, the moving muscles of the horse. And they did that so naturally, with such grace, that the saying among whites was that "the Indian and his horse were one animal."

The Indian did not ride his horse; he became part of his horse and his horse became part of him. It was a natural harmony of man and animal.

Often an Indian would cling to the side of his horse, holding on with nothing but his hands to the horse's mane, with his bare heel hooked on the horse's flank. It was an equestrian style of acrobatics that fascinated nineteenth-century western painters as much as it has twentieth-century western film directors, but its origin was very practical; the Indian horseman, riding in this way, could escape from an enemy by using his horse's body as a shield.

As did so many of the finest horsemen of history, the Indian used his own body to guide his horse. The touch of his thigh or his hand, the slightest twist of his torso let his horse know the direction to go. Sometimes a sort of bridle might be made of a piece of braided cloth or rawhide that was tied around the horse's lower jaw and pulled this way or that to indicate the direction wished.

Most often the Indians rode without a bridle, or saddle, or stirrups, or spurs. They seemed to prefer it that way. In the Battle of Little Big Horn the charismatic Lakota headman, Crazy Horse, was described in a tribal record as riding bareback in pursuit of General Custer though saddles and bridles were available to him; to ride bareback was to be closer to the spirit of your horse, to share its strength.

The one piece of riding gear Indians delighted in using was the lariat. It may have appealed to the sense of sport or pleased the need for muscular grace or excited the esthetic idea of the chase; whatever the reason, in the hands of the Indians the lariat became an instrument of extraordinary skill and of beauty that culminated in the artistry of the Cherokee trick roper by the name of Will Rogers.

In 1805 Lewis and Clark noted in amazement that the Shoshones were "expert at casting the cord about the neck of a running horse." The Nez Percé and Flathead were as proficient in lassoing "exceedingly swift" wild horses. And the Lakota, at about that time, used the lariat as a symbol for wild horses in their history story-paintings, while the Cheyenne, Pawnee, Apache, Assiniboine, Blackfeet, and many other tribes, became famous for their deftness and skill in roping wild horses.

The lasso was like a third hand to the Indian; it was not merely a tool. On capturing a mustang by lassoing it, the rider would throw the animal to the earth, tightening the rope around its neck until it almost choked to death. Then the man would kneel beside the fallen horse and breathe into its nostrils.

It was an ancient way of taming wild beasts by sharing the breath of humans with it, so that it became "human." The man offered his spirit unto the horse.

Once the fallen horse had become somewhat calm, the man tied his legs loosely so that he could stand but not run or kick. The man would then touch the horse with his hand; he would touch him everywhere on his body. Beginning with the face of the horse the man would touch the neck, thighs, legs, flanks, fetlocks and genitals of the frightened animal until it was soothed by the caress of the man's hand. And in that way man and horse came to trust one another. They became like "brothers."

Most of all that brotherhood of man and horse was remarkable because no horses had existed in America since the small, doglike horses of prehistoric times had become extinct ten to twenty thousand years before. The ease and swiftness with which the Indians mastered the horse and the horse accepted the Indians caused them to become, in a few generations, some of the most extraordinary horsemen of history.

In his prophecy of the return of greatness to the native American that holy man of the Oglalla Lakota, Black Elk envisions that horses will herald the resurrection of the people. The horses, he prophesies, will be the sign.

Even though the "poor horse" is quite ordinary,

"the horse is of the earth," he said, "and it is there his power would be used." His horse is "the chief of all the horses"; and "when he snorted it was a flash of lightning and his eyes were like the sunset star." And when the time comes the land would be "filled with a dust of hooves, and horses without number" would be "rejoicing in their fleetness and their strength. It was beautiful, but it was also terrible," he says.

On that day of judgment, in his vision, Black Elk sees four herds of horses of different colors, like the heavenly horses of the Bible, that in Revelation herald the coming reign of justice on earth when the Almighty once more governs humans. But the holy man foresees not the return of the power of God, but the return of the reign of humans and of their horses.

"All the universe was silent, listening; and then the great black stallion raised his voice and sang," Black Elk says, and "the song he sang was this":

> My horses, prancing they are coming.
> My horses, neighing they are coming.
> Prancing, they are coming.
> All over the universe, they come.
> They will dance; may you behold them.
> A horse nation, they will dance. May you behold them.

12 The Passing of the Horse

Men on a horseback—were they the conquerors of the West?

On the long trail of the covered wagon train going West, the pioneers seldom used horses to pull their wagons. They preferred oxen who had more endurance and strength. If the family owned a small herd of horses they usually tied the string behind the wagon, except for one horse that the man of the family pranced around on, while his wife guided the oxen pulling the wagon with the family treasures.

Nonetheless the romantic belief has been that the man on a horse did conquer the West. The clumsy and lumbering oxen hardly evoke an heroic image. Even the nostalgic memory that transforms reality into a legend cannot endow these brutish animals with the majesty and dignity of horses. It's as if one were to suggest replacing the bald eagle with the turkey as our national symbol, as Franklin suggested. But the horse of the pioneer was not all that heroic either. Most often he was a solid and heavy work horse or a farm horse. And his rider was not a dashing cavalier; he was a man of the earth.

Settlers on the frontier were hardly known for their horsemanship. Few had been horsemen back east and most had come west to be farmers, not cowboys; they had a farmer's practical and prosaic view of horses as animals needed for farming, not as symbols of manhood and virility. A settler did not look upon a horse as the cowboy, or *vaquero*, did.

And the horses that they had brought from the East were at first ill-bred to weather the rigors of the rugged climate and terrain of the West. These horses either became acclimatized or they died. They had to be mated with the tough mustangs or Spanish "cow horses" of the open range before they had the strength to survive.

The pioneers who went into the wilderness and their horses were quite similar. Both had to be "Indianized" and "westernized," for going West was a new way of living, a new place on earth, a new philosophy of settling down, making do, and moving on. Nothing was set and permanent as it had been back east.

And a man changed his horses as often as the seasons. In his lifetime a man might ride dozens if not hundreds of different horses. These horses were often nameless (with few exceptions), for a rider would change them so often. Besides, the range was full of mustangs, wild horses to be caught and tamed.

Pony Express riders' style indicated one of the common attitudes toward horses. Some of these riders were famous horsemen, the heroes of the time. They were toasted and celebrated as victorious soldiers who had triumphed over the wilderness by coming through with the mail, and their names are still remembered, names like Clark Foss, Uncle Jim Miller, and Old Charlie. And yet, not even they knew or remembered the names of most of their horses. In his tribute to the daring horsemanship of these men, the historian Oscar Osburn Winther, in *Via Western Express & Stagecoach,* does not mention the name of a single horse. Nor are any horses listed in the index; they do not exist as individual steeds.

Not for their feats of horsemanship but for riding speed were the Pony Express riders rewarded. The fastest riders, not the most graceful or skillful, were most admired. And no one asked them what had happened to their horses along the long trail; their horses seemed to be expendable.

The horses of the old cowboys were "mangy creatures," as one trail boss recalled. But like the "nag" of Don Quixote they did their work and did not complain. The cavalry horse on the frontier was thankful if he made it through the winter without being eaten. Horseflesh was his troops' "favorite meat," said General Crook.

It was rather in the cities of the East that these horses of the West were seen as steeds of the American dream of freedom ever since colonial times. When the would-be gentlemen of New England and the South paradoxically imitated the English aristocrats whom they fought in their fantasies, they saw themselves riding like errant knights upon "Spanish" stallions across the land, much as young George Washington had awed his fellow plantation owners by riding alone through the Indian territory of Ohio.

The noblest horse was always the horse that was farthest from the nearest stable. A horse that ranged wild and free on the prairie was surely the epitome of American virtue and independent will. It represented the democratic spirit.

For the fabled horse of "true Spanish blood" that roamed so freely in the West no "expence in sending them" east was too great, said Governor Patrick Henry of Virginia. And he wrote to his friend Colonel George Rogers Clark, who had set out to explore the Northwest Territory in 1779, that if he found such horses, not to "lose a moment in agreeing to them." Being a good Virginia gentleman he had a stable of fine English horses. No matter, it was those horses of "true Spanish blood" that he dreamt of riding.

The Governor of Virginia knew exactly what he wanted. "Eight Mars" and "Two Horses," he said, who should be "Blood bays, as large as possible, fine Delicate Heads, long Necks, Ears, small and prick'd up near the Ends, Deep Shoulders & Chests, large Arms, well legg'd, Upright pasterns, Clear of Long Hair, Bodys Good, Loins Round, and Very Wide, Out Hock'd, Haunches Straight and Wide behind," he wrote. "There is something so striking and inexpressively beautiful in a fine Horse."

After months of searching in vain for one of these dream horses, Colonel Clark found nothing but the small and scrawny Indian ponies. So he wrote as politely as he could to Patrick Henry: "You have conceived a greater opinion of the Horses in this country than I have."

Dreams do however overshadow reality. And the dream of the "Spanish" horses was as old as the earliest English colonies. On seeing the horses of the conquistadors for the first time in the New World, Sir Walter Raleigh was quoted as saying that they were "the finest horses he ever saw," anywhere.

These horses were supernatural, said William Cavendish, Duke of Newcastle. He thought them "strangely wise beyond any man's imagination" for they knew what a man was thinking without being told; it was devilish clever of those Spaniards. And, he regarded them with an almost religious awe; after all the conquistadors had conquered some of the world's great empires on their backs.

Not nearly as clairvoyant were the horses of England; whether they were elegant thoroughbreds, or mammoth Clydesdales, they were not psychic, mythic, or exotic as the "Spanish" horse was. They merely had good, quite ordinary, English horse sense. The earliest horses brought to the English colonies were imported from Ireland and landed at Jamestown, Virginia, in 1613. But the colonists held them in such lowly esteem that when Captain John Smith returned to England, they ate the herd.

In New England though the first horse, a mare, was recorded in the ownership of Stephen Hopkins in 1632, the Puritans showed little interest in horse breeding until 1685, when they discovered the pleasurable sin of "Jockey-ship" racing, as thoroughbred racing was called. The Puritans were not known for their horses or horsemanship and there were no horses on the Mayflower, for a horse was a symbol in England of the aristocracy, the gentlemen's luxury.

Most of these English horses of the colonists were no more English than the "Spanish" horses were Spanish. Even the proud thoroughbred had been created by mating the English "running mare" with the Berber stallions, the famous Barbs, that had been brought to England in the seventeenth century for that purpose, and when these thoroughbreds were later mated, in the West, to the "Spanish" cow horses, the Berber bloodline was strengthened.

So too the Morgan horse, which originated in Vermont, was not wholly a native breed. It was bred from the colonial quarter horses that were also of Berber origin.

In the mountains and forests of the South, then known as the Spanish *Guale,* the conquistadors had begun to raise horses in great numbers from their earliest expeditions. By 1650 these Spaniards had established seventy-nine Catholic missions, eight large towns and two royal ranches in Florida and along the Gulf coastline. From these settlements many hundreds of horses began to wander north into the English colonies.

And it was these "Spanish" or Berber horses that became the basis for the herds that the Cherokees and Chickasaws raised so expertly. Within a few generations both tribes had become famous as horse breeders. Their horses were "the most highly regarded as saddle horses," wrote Dr. John Irving who visited the tribes in 1754. J. F. D. Smyth, who had journeyed through the Indian villages in 1784, commented that they "have a beautiful breed of horses amongst them—which they preserve unmixed"; but if these horses were bred with English horses, they produced foals of "great beauty and speed." And these Indian-bred Berber horses, Barbs renamed Chickasaws, became one of the most sought after saddle and racehorse breeds on the plains, where they were mated with the "Spanish" cow horse and became a favorite of the cowboys.

Berber and Indian horses thus became the forebears of "most western breeds," says Richard Denhardt in *The Horse of the Americas.* The venerable authority on western horses, General W. Tweedle, puts it more bluntly—the cowboy horse was nothing but an "African Arab," he says. And Frank Dobie adds to that: "The Spanish horse was a *mestizo.*"

On the plains of the West the original horsemen shared the same origin as their horses. They shared a horse culture. The old cowboy of the West "did not exist as an American [Yankee] type," the artist of the West Frederick Remington once said: "Don't mistake those nice young men who amble around wire fences with the 'old rider of the Plains.' " In the old days the cowboys were mostly Mexicans and Indians. Remington said: "You want to credit the Mexican with the whole business."

Remington's sharp words were in response to an enquiry from Owen Wister, author of that western classic *The Virginian.* In 1884, the editor of *Harper's New Monthly Magazine* asked Wister to write an article, "The Evolution and Survival of the Cowboy," and Wister asked Remington for advice. When "The Evolution of the Cow Puncher" finally appeared in 1895 the word "survival" had been taken out of the title, and Wister remembered Remington's harsh words. "Let it be remembered," Wister writes, "that the Mexican was the original cowboy" and the Easterners merely had "improved on him."

The old teller of horse tales, Philip Ashton Rollins, in *The Cowboy,* many years later portrays the oldtime *vaqueros* in the same way: "To the Mexicans the American cowboy owed his vocation," Rollins writes. "He obtained from Mexican sources all the tools of his trade, all the technics of his craft, the very words by which he designed his utensils, the very animals he dealt with . . ."

And yet, acknowledging the cowboy's debt to the Mexican and the Indian, Rollins then denies its past existence and present relevance by saying: "For his character [the cowboy] was indebted to no one. As one of the dominant figures in the development of the United States he was self-made."

Most recently, in *The Last Cowboy* by *New Yorker* writer Jane Kramer, the history of the horsemen and horses of the West has been eliminated by a single sentence: "Like the frontier, he [the cowboy] has no past and no history." The cowboy invented himself from the fantasies of Hollywood movies he has seen, Kramer writes. He never really existed.

So the histories of the nineteenth century were rewritten in the twentieth. It was not that the heritage of those dark and dashing horsemen has been forgotten and lost; it has been denied and tossed aside by its heirs. Once that was done history could easily be turned into a fantasy, completely undressed and then reclothed in contemporary dreams.

Now that the horse has lost its importance in life, it has loomed even larger in memory; and it has been endowed with a history and nobility it never possessed.

In 1874 in his eulogy for the death of

horsemanship in the West entitled *The World on Wheels,* Benjamin Taylor does not mourn. He is ecstatic in his praise of the horses' successor, the Iron Horse, the "consolidated arm of Christendom" as he names it; the "Spiritual aspiration" of the entire nation rode in its carriages. The Iron Horse was a "civilizer," it was "the Angel of Abundance," it was "the cunning right hand of mankind" that "brought the world to the wilderness" and "brought the Gentiles" to "whistle that barbarism of the Orient down the wind."

"There was no train to Jerusalem," Taylor explains "and the Lord of Life rode into the city in the humblest guise—upon a donkey." No longer would the citizens have to ride as Jesus did. They now could ride the Iron Horse right unto the Star of Bethlehem, wrote Taylor; surely, this was the path to heaven and "the untrodden pastures of God" riding "from Providence to the Golden Gate." God rides the Iron Horse, says Taylor, to "Solomon's Temple" in the West.

It was fitting that the first western movie was *The Great Train Robbery* whose real hero was an Iron Horse, while the horsemen of the West were reduced to thieves who sought to overpower it. It is fitting too that in one of the first westerns made by William Hart, when the script called for a horse to jump from a cliff and the horse refused, they built a mechanical horse to do what the real horse would not.

And so began that long trail that led to the mechanical horse of John Travolta in *The Urban Cowboy*. On the ranches of the West nowadays, they roundup cattle with a Jeep or a Toyota (called the "Tokyo quarter horse").

The myth of the western horsemen has been mechanized. And shorn of its history it has become a fantasy that has grown larger than life as the work of horses has diminished. The white man upon the white horse, the Lone Ranger on our dream frontier, has replaced the dark and dashing horsemen, the Mexicans and the Indians, on their "African Arab" horses of the West, much as the Iron Horse replaced the real one.

No one remembers the name of Daniel Boone's horse. For that matter who now recalls the names of the horses ridden by Paul Revere, George Washington, Lewis and Clark, Zebulon Pike, Sam Houston, Jesse James, Billy the Kid, Joaquin Murieta, Santa Anna, Geronimo, Sitting Bull, General Custer, Crazy Horse, Manuelito, Black Elk, or even Owen Wister?

And yet, everybody remembers the Lone Ranger's horse, Silver, and Roy Rogers's horse, Trigger.

Epilogue: The White Steed of the Prairies

On the prairies there appeared the Phantom Horse of the West, the Ghostly Horse of the Plains, the Vision Horse of the Lakota Nation, the Rainbow Horse of the Navajo, the Iron Horse of the railroad companies, the Great White Horse Silver of the Lone Ranger, the White Steed of the Prairie.

He has had many names.

In one thousand places and in one thousand guises the White Steed has been seen. He has been reported on the Brazos River in Texas and in the High Sierras of California. For nearly a century he has ranged over the prairies and the mountains of the West as an apparition. No one has ever captured him. No one ever will. One cannot saddle and ride a vision.

To the horsemen of the West the dream of a perfect horse was satisfying enough. But in the East the writers of the past had to determine whether the mysterious horse existed in myth or in the flesh. They had to know whether the wild horse that no one could tame was real, or a fantasy, or both.

Perhaps the first appearance of the White Steed in the East came in Washington Irving's *A Tour on the Prairies*. On camping on the banks of the Arkansas River in 1832, the writer hears tell of a "famous grey horse" who roams the wild range, a horse so fast he cannot be caught because he is "faster than the fleetest horse" alive—a tale that Irving dismisses as a legend, a tall tale of the West.

"The old hunters tell of a large white horse [who] roams his native prairies in freedom, always alone," the trader George Kendall, wrote in *Narrative of the Texas Santa Fe Expedition* in 1841. He believed it. Not only was this horse so fast he could never be caught, he "was far superior in form, and action, to any of his brothers." And in 1844, Josiah Gregg in his *Commerce on the Prairies* confirmed that he too heard "marvelous tales" of a "mustang stallion of perfect symmetry, milk white," whom many men had seen but none could catch.

Ballads to the "White Steed" began to appear in the East. This one, published in a magazine in New

York in 1843, must have titillated the urban
cowboys of the day:

> Fleet barb of the prairie,
> in vain they prepare
> For thy neck, arched in beauty,
> the treacherous snare.
> Thou wilt toss thy proud head,
> and nostrils stretched wide,
> Defy them again,
> as thou still hast defied.

> Not the team of the Sun,
> as in fable portrayed,
> Through the firmament rushing
> in glory arrayed,
> Could match in wild majesty,
> beauty and speed,
> That tireless, magnificent,
> snowy-white steed.

For years after, hundreds of stories of the
"White Steed" appeared in the magazines and
books published in the East. But the authors could
not seem to capture the spirit of the fabled horse,
perhaps because they did not seem to know what
they were looking for.

Of those many one man alone seemed to know.
Though he had never seen a wild horse or talked
to a western horseman, he alone captured the spirit

of the "White Steed." His name was Herman Melville.

In *Moby Dick,* a book supposedly about the sea, which he likens to the endless prairie, Melville compares the seaman's unachievable quest for the conquest of the evil and ecstasy of nature in the image of the white whale, Moby Dick, to the pursuit of the White Steed. He, too, could never be caught. Melville, in the remarkable chapter "The Whiteness of the Whale," seeks to learn the meaning of perfect and terrible whiteness in the stories that have been written of that quest.

Of these stories Melville writes:

Most famous in our western and Indian traditions is that of the White Steed of the Prairies; a magnificent milk-white charger, large-eyed, small-headed, bluff-chested, and with the dignity of a thousand monarchs in his lofty, over-scorning carriage. He was the elected Xerxes of the vast herds of wild horses, whose pastures in those days were only fenced by the Rocky Mountains and the Alleghenies. At their flaming head he westward trooped it like the chosen star which each evening leads on the host of lights.

The horse is "a most imperial and archangelic apparition," Melville writes, "of that unfallen, western world." He is a new sort of angel in a new garden, before the fall from grace once more of humans; and he is the archangel of the Lord's judgment as well.

Once more the horse became a messenger of God; "he revived the glories of those primeval times when Adam walked majestic as a god, fearless as this mighty steed," Melville says. For, this horse was "clothed in divineness."

Longing to ride on the White Steed, thousands sought him, but none found him. It was no more possible for them to capture him, than it was for them to recapture their lost innocence. Though many wished to become the man on the white horse, none were to succeed.

That may be what was so wonderous and ominous about him; he was Moby Dick of the Prairies, the White Steed that no man dared ride but at his own peril. For if a man succeeded he would surely be ridden to his death, and worse than that, the death of his fantasy.

And so, no one ever rode upon the White Steed. He alone among horses will forever be free.